"Julie Lavata's book is a [...] her husband John's journey to [...] safe haven law allowing a bi [...] her newborn, Julie and John [...] ntil they could welcome a child into their home. Hopefully more women in crisis pregnancies will learn about the safe haven law's message and infant abandonment will cease.

Adoption is a selfless and loving act. The courage of Halle's birthmother has created a new living family which will always cherish and be grateful to a woman who chose her child's happiness and security through a safe haven adoption.

This story encapsulates the true events I have seen time and time again of two people who finally find the child they have so desperately wanted."

—*Timothy Jaccard*
President/Director of AMT Children of Hope Baby Safe Haven Foundation and Founding Board member of the National Safe Haven Alliance

"Some stories need to be heard. Fire Station Baby is one of those stories. Adoption is not for the faint of heart, I know, we've been down that road. But, in the midst of that journey, we find beauty and grace that we would never have experienced otherwise. There is magic and hope in this story that will follow you long after you're done reading."

—*Danny Oertli, Singer/Author*

"Fire Station Baby is an intimate portrayal of the lives of two of our friends who have endured more than most. It's an authentic portrayal of their journey through the heartbreak of infertility and then through the many twists and turns of the adoption process of foster children. Julie weaves her thoughts in a way that every parent who has been a part of a similar journey will want to hear. Julie and John's faith remained strong in times of desperation and together they refused to give up even though it cost them thousands of tears along the way. Rob and I are proud to be their friends and have rejoiced with them as their family grew. For us, the story is even more tender because Rob was adopted and we're able to relate to the joy their children will have from being placed in a loving home with parents who literally did whatever it took to make them their own. Fire Station Baby will make you laugh, cry and really begin to think about adoption in a way you haven't before. It's filled with grit, real life, and an abundance of emotion that enables a person to really feel the depths of pain and joy that comes, sometimes at great cost, with becoming a parent."

—*Pastor Rob and Carol Ann Kelly (Rob is the lead pastor at Northern Hills Church in Brighton, Colorado)*

"I am thrilled to recommend this book to you. I laughed through my tears as Julie's wit wove through the honest and often painful details of her journey of adoption. Never before have I been able to empathize so deeply with women who are going through similar struggles. Julie's descriptions ignited within me a level of compassion that could only be surpassed by someone who has been down this long and bumpy road themselves. It will be on the top of my list of recommendations for anyone dealing with infertility or thinking of adopting."

—*Anita Baumgartner, Parker, Colorado*
Ladies group leader and pastor's wife

"This is a heart-stretching book that draws you in to the ebb & flow of adoption, being transparent even when it hurts. The author shares the most intimate moments where a precious child is held so close to her heart, but far from her own! Although adoption is not for the faint of heart, Julie freely shares her journey as a mother and an advocate for children of adoption and foster care. You will be touched. Your heart will be changed. I promise."
—*Pam Sweet-Wilson, grandma of three beautiful granddaughters, two of whom were adopted through foster care*

"This is exactly the kind of story we hoped to see from the Safe Haven Law."
—*Pam Rhodes, former Colorado State Representative*

"This book & the entire story behind it has had such a dramatic impact on my life and that of my entire family. It is the heart and soul of life, love, loss and happiness for Julie. Her story pulls the readers in immediately and each page leaves us waiting to see what will happen next as we muster thru the tears we share for each step of sorrow and joy. Julie's journey is not just about her, but about every child out there in need of a forever home, a forever family - to become a forever child. Julie's passion brought our own family to foster care and eventually adoption. For her and her story, I am forever grateful and a changed person."

—*Corinne McMurray (myself adopted as an infant) mother of 4 children, the oldest adopted thru the Foster Adopt program.*

"Fire Station Baby is one of those books that pulls you in and doesn't let go of you until the last page. Julie's story will have you laughing and in tears. She has a wonderful way with words. This book is not to be missed!"

—*Jane Karel, adoptive aunt*

"God's plan for our lives is often not the easiest. Nor is it what we may have expected. This book is a journey full of heartache, disappointment and complete joy as God grows their family --and their faith-- through adoption. We were so blessed to see the Burke's heart remain faithful and strong as they pressed on to find real treasures (often hidden) and love that God had waiting for them......children to call their own. We highly recommend this book and journey to you."

—*Scott & Wendi Smith (Parents to 4 biological children and 6 adopted children from China.)*

"I love, Love, LOVE your adoption story!"

—*Cara Barnett, adoptee and mother of two*

"I know [Fire Station Baby] will give couples hope."
—*Tiffany Ewing*

"This is a book that so intensely depicts the power of human emotion. As Julie invites you to walk with her through the highs and lows of adoption, she reveals expression that is riveting, informative and life changing. She is an incredible influencer. Julie inspires others to choose the high road of human value, extending the hands of extraordinary love and favor. Embrace this life changing book by letting it be a part of your emotions and thoughts."
—*Garald and Cara Pugh, Pastors and Grandparents of 8*

FIRE STATION BABY

Where Faith
Became a Family

JULIE LAVATA

For my husband and daughter —

No father and daughter have ever been more perfectly paired.
When God made you, He matched you.

In Memory Of

My Dad
You took me to Sunday school and taught me about Jesus…
by example.

and

My Mom
Generous, loving, honest and fun, you were my best girl friend.
In your absence, the colors in my world have dimmed.

Table of Contents

Acknowledgements

This book wouldn't even have been possible without the mentorship and guidance of Doug Schmidt. He taught me how to begin writing and directed me each step of the way. He was my teacher, editor, mentor, accountability partner—and along with his lovely wife, Dawna—my psycho-therapist. He gave selflessly of his time and talents and I am truly and deeply grateful.

The following people were early endorsers and readers of the manuscript. Their wonderful, kind words kept me going. In no particular order, I want to thank Anita Baumgartner, Rob and Carol Ann Kelly, Danny Oertli, Pam Wilson, Garald and Cara Lynn Pugh, Cara Barnett, Scott and Wendi Smith, Corinne McMurray, Jane Karel, Kari Roff, Chris Sveum, Tiffany Ewing and Pam Rhodes.

Sometimes all it takes to make a child feel extra special is a welcomed hug, a shared smile or a knowing wink when you meet. These sweet ladies did that for my daughter. Peggy Black was the first person outside of my immediate family that I wanted to meet my baby. She adored her from the beginning and has showered her with hugs and gifts and love throughout the years. Additionally, Theresa Gilbreath was an early childhood Sunday school teacher and VBS leader whose gift with children was obvious. Her special smile and hug for my daughter made her glow for the rest of the day. And finally, Arlene Masterson was the first to teach my daughter how to make and respect friends her own age. She was also the first to whom I entrusted my child's education. By making my daughter feel special, they all have won a special place in my heart as well.

When I first thought I had been led to write this book, I told one friend, Roisin Stukas. Sharing your dreams with other people is a scary thing, but Roisin was wonderfully encouraging. She also kept it to herself until I was ready to move forward.

The summer before she had gotten sick, I mentioned my idea about this book to my mom. She loved it! A few months later when she was rehabbing between strokes, she would ask me how the book was coming. She couldn't remember what year it was, but she remembered to tell me to get it written. I loved her for that.

My sisters, Kathy and Mary, have been wonderfully supportive. They and their daughters—Bria and Julia and Quinna and Ryann—have been readers and "cheer-readers" from the beginning. I loved it when you called me up and shared a memory or commented on a post. And I want to send a special thank you to Quinna and Ryann for babysitting my children all these years. I have loved that they spent that time with their cousins. I love you all.

Finally, I am grateful for my beautiful children who fill my days with happy chaos and for the man who makes it all possible for me. My husband and best friend, John, has read my first drafts, my re-writes and my re-rewrites with equal enthusiasm. He is my biggest "cheer-reader" of all. I love you.

Introduction

Dear Birth Mother,

In life, there are only a few times an event or circumstance will change your path. For me, one was the cold, February evening you surrendered your baby to the fire station. You secured her safety and survival under the Safe Haven Law, which was largely unknown back then. And although I didn't know it at the time, you set into motion the events that would culminate in my becoming a mother. For that, I am grateful.

We have always told her that she was adopted and explained that her birth mother loved her so much that she made sure she was safe and cared for. Around our house, the story has been told so often it has become somewhat mythological.

But she is at an age now where she is asking questions. She wants to know if she looks like you and if she will ever meet you, but mostly, she wants to know why. What happened that you couldn't care for her and why did you give her up? I wonder myself sometimes.

You cannot possibly know, but you did something for me that I could not do for myself. Your unselfish decision to deliver and then give up your baby allowed me to become a mom—the one thing I always knew I wanted—and for that, I feel deeply bonded to you. I cannot fathom what you must have endured inwardly and outwardly when you gave up your baby. I imagine it was only heartwrenching. Please know that you are my personal hero, and that at our house, you are held in high esteem.

This book details my journey to adopting the baby girl you took to the fire station those years ago. This book is also a praise to God from whom every blessing flows and a thank you to you, who I believe obeyed a call. Finally, it is a keepsake for the little girl to know what her parents went through to build a family.

I hope you enjoy it!

Chapter 1
IUI? IVF? OMG!

"We don't know why you're not getting pregnant." The doctor pressed his hands together and steepled his index fingers below his chin.

I thought back to that first IUI (intrauterine insemination) six months before. I was so nervous, yet hopeful, as I sat in the waiting room. An attractive, young nurse called me back and led me to a procedure room. "Have a seat," she instructed. "Another nurse will be in shortly."

John was in earlier in the day to "deposit his sample," as they called it. From there, the deposit was shaken, stirred, and spun into the most fertile concoction of sperm mobility and motility possible. It would then be inseminated into my uterus and hopefully, we'd soon be expecting. Honestly, the lengths people will go to conceive! It wasn't even private anymore.

As I sat waiting, another young, pretty nurse rolled an ultrasound machine into the room and explained that they used ultrasound to guide the tubing to the top of the uterus where the insemination had the highest probability of conception.

As I opened my mouth to remark about the irony of conceiving without my husband in the room, a third nurse bounced into the room with the "deposit." She was even more stunning than the first two. *Was physical perfection required to work here?* Tall, tan, blonde, and fit, RN Barbie spoke alarmingly fast and high-pitched. She squeaked on and on about the excellence of John's sperm and how important that was in the process.

Just as my discomfort reached its peak, a doctor—not mine—came in with the nurse who greeted me, sorority sister #1. She would take notes while sorority sister #2 ran the ultrasound machine and RN Barbie assisted the doctor. I was having a bad body-image day.

I laid back and we began. Each of the nurses assured me that everything was going well, and if sheer words were enough, the five of us in the room would have willed me pregnant.

Two weeks later, though, I learned that I wasn't. That cycle continued for five more months and at month number three, we added fertility drugs to the mix.

The doctor had broken into my thoughts with his new plan: in vitro fertilization (IVF). He explained that there would be a series of stronger, injectable fertility drugs that would cause me to produce several eggs. Those eggs would then be harvested and fertilized in a petri dish. Based on my age and health, he estimated that there would be at least a dozen or more resulting embryos. At that point, we would implant one or two per cycle and freeze the rest. Hopefully, the first attempt would be successful, but if not, we'd repeat the process every month until we were. Oh, and by the way, each attempt costs $12,000. He slid a sheet of paper across the desk. It listed the banks that granted loans for just such fertility treatments.

I was shocked! *Frozen babies? Stronger drugs? Twelve thousand dollars per month?*

He mistook my horror for confusion and asked if we had questions or were we ready to get started? I told him no, shot John the eye, and announced that we would have to think about this. That was John's cue to get up and leave, which he executed perfectly.

This whole new plan was overwhelming. For me, there were more red flags going up than at sunrise in Beijing.

Chapter 2
Too Many Concerns

After leaving the fertility clinic, we jumped into the car for the thirty-minute ride home. John knew something was nagging at me and waited to hear what it was. Truth be told, he didn't even need to ask. By then, he knew me well enough to know he would hear about it anyway.

I narrowed my concerns down to three areas. The first was my emotional state. I had been taking the fertility drug Clomid for three months, and while it had improved and regulated my ovulation, my moods declined and I was highly irritable. How was I going to handle the more potent, injectable drugs? I worked two part-time jobs during that period, and on the days I was home, John regularly checked-in with me around lunchtime. If he happened to call while I was sleeping, I accused him of being inconsiderate for waking me. And if he didn't call, I would attack him for not caring. He couldn't win. One evening, he brought home takeout. But, he dared to get the same entrée I got! *How could he do such a thing? We always got two different dinners so we could share each other's food and sample a little variety. What was he thinking? Surely he was doing this to spite me!* I ate in silence and stormed off to bed immediately after dinner. Little issues set me off, but big issues paralyzed me altogether. The worst of it came when it was time to take the pregnancy test. Every month, I would convince myself that I was pregnant and that the treatments worked this time—I just knew. Each pregnancy test I took at home would return a negative result, but I insisted on going down to the fertility clinic for a blood test anyway. *Those things are only 99 percent accurate, right?* I extended my hope for a few more hours. Then the nurse would call with the bad news. I would hang up, navigate the stairs as best I could through the sobs, and fall into bed, where I would let the salty tears run freely off my face until the pillowcase was soaked. And at some point, I would fall asleep.

My second concern was financial. I was a frugal girl. It wasn't that I had never taken out a loan, but I had paid them off as quickly as I could. My Mom always said to pay a little more each month on the principal and get the loan paid off quickly, so when John and I got married and he brought debt to the marriage, it was important for me to get rid of it as soon as we could. In fact, we had used the money we received as gifts from our wedding to pay off our outstanding credit cards. Don't think for a moment that that didn't rankle! About a year later, my boss had loaned me a copy of Dave Ramsey's Financial Peace Revisited and I was on a new mission. Over the next eighteen months, we paid off all $30,000 of John's student loans. So, I might have been persuaded to take a $12,000 per month loan for the IVF, but there was no guarantee that it would work, and we had no idea how many months it might take to work. And, if it didn't work at all, I'd still have the debt. Furthermore, when we did have children, I wanted to get rid of at least one of the part-time jobs and be at home a little more. We would have less income to pay off the loans. No, for me, it was too risky.

Finally, my third concern was moral. Let's say, hypothetically, the IVF did work and that I somehow survived the drugs, twelve eggs were successfully harvested, and they all fertilized. We would only implant two at the most. What then? Freeze the embryos? *Frozen babies?* We didn't want twelve children. We each came from families with three children. That was our goal. Why did freezing the embryos bother me so badly? In my mind, it was like having babies out there waiting to be born, but they never would be. They would be frozen forever unless someone else wanted to carry them to term as her own child. But what was the likelihood that a couple would go through all the expense and emotion of the IVF process just to use our embryos? Probably not high. And donating them to research was out of the question for me as well. I wouldn't give my child away to science, why would I give my embryos? They were living beings. It was too personal for me, and I struggled with the morality of it all.

John agreed that there were some concerns and suggested that we seek the advice of our pastor. Maybe he would have some ideas. Maybe after counseling with him, we would have some clarity.

Chapter 3
Seeking Counsel

I believe that even in the busyness of everyday life, whether you know it or not at the time, a simple conversation can redirect your focus and take you in a different direction. For me, looking back, I know the conversation with our pastor was one of those encounters. Why John suggested that we counsel with the lead pastor of our church, Dennis, is still unknown to me. There was at least one other staff pastor that we knew better and with whom we were on more casual terms.

For my part, I saw only two options. One was adoption, which I knew from research there was a fee of about $25,000 for newborn babies and an indeterminable waiting period. The other was IVF, which of course cost $12,000 per month for treatments, and there was no guarantee how long it might take to work. It seemed that debt was our fate in either scenario, and given that, my preference was to have a biological child. Therefore, I was hoping to be absolved of the guilt I felt about IVF.

When we arrived at our pastor's office, I took a seat in the chair and John sat at the corner of the couch nearest me. Dennis was at his desk. Dennis joked that he knew we weren't newlyweds because they always sat on the same cushion of the couch, nearly on top of one another. It was nearly sickening, he laughed and crinkled up his nose.

We all chatted for a few minutes, and then Dennis asked how he could help today.

I began by giving Dennis a brief history about what we had been through between fertility testing and treatments and the crossroads where we now found ourselves with IVF. John interjected that we felt uneasy about freezing embryos and asked Dennis what he would suggest we do?

Dennis was quick to respond. He suggested that we adopt. He said that there were so many children from all around the world who needed good homes. We could give a child the chance at a better life. He shared with us that his sister had adopted two beautiful children from Central America and they were adjusting well to their new lives. Many other church members had chosen to adopt and were happy that they did. He went on to suggest that another option could be to carry another couple's embryos and deliver them as we would a biological child. It would be adopting a baby at an earlier stage.

That gave us something else to consider.

As we wrapped up our meeting, Dennis prayed over us for clarity in the decisions we would be making and perseverance over the obstacles we were facing.

It was only when we got to the car that I realized he never recommended IVF as an option. And if we went to the trouble of seeking his advice, why would we ignore it? IVF was officially off the table as an option and that solved my moral and emotional issues, but I wasn't quite ready to take a loan and spend $25,000 to adopt one baby. I wasn't sure what we would do now.

Chapter 4
A Seed Is Planted

Weeks after counseling with our pastor, I was still unsure of how to proceed. At least one of my original three concerns was still an issue in any of our foreseeable options. If we chose IVF, which was now not an option after speaking with our pastor, I worried about the emotional, moral, and financial aspects. If we chose private adoption, the financial burden would still be an obstacle, especially if we wanted more than one child, which we did.

During that time, I felt paralyzed by indecision. Surely there was an option that didn't cripple us financially. Certainly, if we were trying so hard to be obedient to God's Word, we wouldn't be led into debt. *Is there any verse in the Bible that says debt is a blessing?* Sure, we might be tried emotionally, but it wouldn't be as a result of synthetic drugs. I knew the answer would come to us, but in the meantime, I spent hours on the couch watching dust motes float in the ribbons of sunlight that beamed through the living-room window. The dust motes never seemed to land, and likewise, my conversations with God never seemed to end as we waited for answers about our baby.

One Sunday, weeks later, we headed to my mom's house for lunch. Sunday lunch at Mom's house was legendary. She had hosted this affair for years and enjoyed it so much. When we were teenagers, our friends and youth groups would come and eat. When we were dating, our boyfriends enjoyed the afternoon at her table, and now that we were all married, our husbands and her grandchildren benefited from her hospitality and generosity. Comfort food was always on the menu, usually featuring steak, roast, or ham with creamy mashed potatoes, gravy, crusty French bread, real butter, and some other starchy vegetable followed by dessert.

That particular Sunday afternoon, my sisters and I retired to Mom's bedroom in a near-comatose state after lunch. We all laid on her bed, like we did when we were younger, and talked. I told them about the fertility tests, how we were struggling with what to do next, and in general, how we were at a standstill.

My younger sister reiterated her offer to be a surrogate for us. She even offered to let us use her eggs if that would make it less expensive for us. The offer was so kind, of course, but how do you tell your child that Aunt Mary carried you in her belly, not Mommy. For that matter, half of your chromosomes are from Aunt Mary and half are from Dad. Confusing and weird! *Like "I'm My Own Grandpa" country-song weird!* Anyway, her offer made me giggle a little. This was the sister who never let me into her room to play with her toys. This was the sister who to that day had never let me touch her prized Cabbage Patch dolls, and here she was offering me her uterus!

I looked impishly at my older sister, Kathy. She immediately shot down any thoughts I might have had about her being a surrogate. She reminded me that carrying her own two daughters was difficult for her, and her second baby arrived just in time. Turns out, she was suffering from placental abruption. Another pregnancy was discouraged, as her risks for another placental abruption were higher. Again, I marveled at the irony. Mary, who wouldn't share her room, her toys, or her dolls was offering me the use of her uterus. And Kathy, who to this day has given me her Coach bags, shoes, furniture, wall hangings, makeup, and one car, finally drew the line at her uterus! I loved these women, and I relied on their support.

Kathy did, however, offer a suggestion. She suggested that I look into possibly adopting through foster care. I told her that we wanted an infant. Weren't the children in foster care older? She said she knew one of the patients at the dental office where she worked had adopted several babies through foster care. And I should look into it.

Yes, I should. And yes, I would, first thing Monday morning.

Chapter 5
No Such Thing As Coincidence

We left Mom's house to attend a service at church that evening. I could hardly contain my excitement at the possibility that we could adopt a newborn baby without spending tens of thousands of dollars. All of a sudden, visions of swaddled babies danced in my head!

We arrived just after the service started and took our seats in the back. The band began to play and I sang and peeped as the even-later arrivals trickled in. I was always amazed at how some of the late arrivals made their way to the front of the sanctuary. Was it because there were no seats left in the back, or because they wanted to be seen by everyone? Or was it some other reason entirely? To me, coming in late and being forced to the front of the church was akin to the walk of shame. And I had been there more than once.

One couple in particular, however, caught my attention. A couple we knew casually, Will and Sarah, had raced in and taken seats in the back on the other side of the sanctuary. What caught my eye was that Will was carrying a car seat. That meant they had a baby! How did that happen? Sarah hadn't been pregnant. They had one handsome little son who was about five years old, but no other children. So, where did they get the baby?

I poked John on the arm and pointed in their direction. "Where did Will and Sarah get that baby?" I whispered. It was part question and part accusation. What I was asking was twofold: 1) Were they adopting a baby? And 2) Did John know about it and forget to tell me? John sometimes neglected to tell me crucial information, absolutely sure that he thought he did. Was this one of those times? All of that was implied in one simple question, and John understood completely. His simple "I don't know" cleared up both questions, as did his look of interest in the baby.

I am ashamed to say that I didn't hear one word of the sermon. My mind was focused on the baby in that car seat. I kept glancing over to see if they were holding the baby. But they weren't. Of all the bad luck! That baby slept through the entire service in the car seat.

I must not have been the only curious observer because a group of looky-loos gathered around Sarah after the service. She pulled out the beautiful baby girl and passed her around for all the women to hold. She was such a sweet baby, never minding being caressed and kissed and unwrapped by each woman. She was only a week old. Sarah explained that baby Emma would be adopted as soon as possible because both biological parents had signed over their parental rights to her.

When I asked her what agency she went through, she replied, "Foster care, through the county."

I thought my heart would explode! There it was, right before me in the flesh! A sign!

Chapter 6
Calling All Counties

Monday morning arrived, and I was on a mission. Energized and armed with the phone book, I was going to find out how adopting through foster care worked. So, I called every county in the Denver Metro area. I guess I was trying to find the quickest way possible to adopt a baby, but who really knows what I was thinking? I was desperate, so I decided that being rational was optional. I left several messages, but got to speak live to three counties.

The first county, where I secretly desired to live, didn't work with couples outside their county. In fact, the caseworker explained, most of the children brought into foster care in their county were reunited with their parents. So, they really didn't have a need for adoptive parents. Thank you for calling and bye-bye.

I asked the second caseworker I spoke with if they placed newborn babies for adoption. Her response was that they considered "infants" to mean any children up to one year old. She couldn't promise that we would be placed with a newborn. Well, that wasn't my preference, but it was certainly an option if we couldn't adopt a newborn baby elsewhere. She was polite and invited me to call back if we were interested in pursuing an adoption through them.

At that point, I was getting frustrated and a little sad. So far, the only option was adopting a baby who could be up to one year old. When we had discussed it, we had decided that a newborn was what we wanted. At least for the first one. We wanted to experience all the stages of infancy. Babies grow and change so much the first year, and we felt that by adopting a one year old, we would be missing out on so many milestones. I was surprised at how quickly despair was creeping up on me. I seemed to land there a lot during my infertility ride, and I was now back there again.

I headed up the stairs to lie on the bed and cry my eyes out. It had become a ritual. Every time one of my friends announced her pregnancy or a lady from church presented her newborn, I would genuinely congratulate her and then head home to feel sorry for myself. It was happening a lot. To me, it seemed like there was a baby boom. Like it was nine months after an early March blizzard that had kept everyone shut in for three days. Women were getting pregnant whether they wanted to or not. Before I hit the bed, the phone rang. It was another caseworker returning my call. She introduced herself as Karen. When I asked her to explain their foster to adoption program, she responded by asking me questions. *Was this a kinship adoption? How did we hear about foster to adopt? What ages were we interested in? Were we interested in sibling groups?*

I got direct with her, figuring her answer would be somewhere between the first two counties. I said, look, we wanted to adopt a newborn baby, but we were financially strapped from months of infertility testing and treatments. Was that possible and how long might it take?

She must have fielded questions like those from many desperate couples, because she calmly replied that yes, they placed newborns all the time and it could take anywhere from weeks to months from the time we became certified. Hard to say, of course. She spent the next ten minutes talking about their program and answering my other questions and then ended by inviting us to an introduction class later that month.

I didn't know if it was that she had given me the hope I was looking for, or if it was her warm and engaging personality, but at that moment, I trusted her completely. I trusted she would help us build our family.

Chapter 7
Previewing the Madness

We arrived at the county building and found the assigned room for the class. The color of the room must have been chosen from a swatch that was called "Interrogation Room Blue," because that was the color of the walls with dark-blue flecked commercial carpet, which was a surprise to me. I thought all government buildings were painted some shade of soothing taupe. Maybe it seemed like an interrogation room because, despite the fluorescent lighting, the room was badly lit and shadowy in spots. It was two rooms, actually, that were separated by accordion doors that had been pulled to the side to create one large, functional room. Tables were pushed together in the shape of a horseshoe, and at the near side of the room was a whiteboard where the instructor set her supplies. Chairs were set up on the periphery of the horseshoe and at the far end was a lone table with cookies, coffee, pop, and water.

We were greeted by Karen, who asked us to sign in, grab some refreshments, and have a seat. As usual, the seats at the back of the room filled up first, and the unfortunate latecomers would have to take the chairs at the front with Karen.

Karen started the meeting by introducing herself as the Adoption Recruiter and Trainer for the county. For sixteen years she had been in that position and had seen many families created through the adoption process. To start, she wanted to go around the room and have everyone introduce themselves, give their professions, and indicate what aged child they were interested in adopting. I assumed everyone was there to adopt a newborn baby, but in fact, that was not the case. In the room of about twenty-four people, about half wanted newborn babies, but some wanted sibling groups, a few wanted a specific gender because they already had biological children of the other gender, and one lady was there to adopt her grandchild.

Karen gave an overview of the "legal risk" program by explaining that we all would become certified foster parents with the intent to adopt. When we accepted a child for placement, the county would ask that we commit to adopt that child if and/or when he became legally free for adoption. However, sometimes there was risk to us as foster parents as the child may not become free for adoption. In that case, the child would be reunified with his biological parents. We, as foster parents, were asked to take on that risk for the sake of the child. Children who were moved from placement to placement were more likely to develop attachment disorders, so the county's goal was to place them only once, if possible.

On the flip side, if the child became legally free for adoption, the foster parents, already having a bond with the child, would be the first choice of the county to adopt him for the cost of court fees only.

She explained that because the children they took in were abused or neglected, sometimes the placements happened on short notice. They would try to give us as much information as possible, but sometimes they just didn't have it when they asked us to make a decision. Fortunately, most of the children they placed were healthy, despite the abuse or neglect. And statistically speaking, only about 8 percent of the children placed in "legal risk" foster homes experienced a disruption that sent them back to their biological parents.

Karen went on to give a cross section of the population of the county and how it mostly mirrored the races of children the county took in. She, of course, could not guarantee any time limit for placement, but she did say that the more flexible we were with gender, age, and race, the faster we would be placed. She finished up the forty-five-minute meeting on time as promised and invited everyone to return for the foster parent certification classes that, conveniently, began the next week. If we had questions, we were invited to stay after and ask her. Otherwise, we could address them at the classes.

As John and I left, we decided to commit to the certification classes. But for me, there was one nagging question. I understood what it meant to neglect a newborn. But what did it mean to abuse a newborn baby?

My imagination ran wild. I thought up many scenarios. And every scenario I could think up was worse than the one before.

Chapter 8
Overwhelming Thoughts

The morning after our introduction class, some issues still bothered me. If infants are taken into custody by social services because of abuse or neglect, what does it mean to abuse a newborn? And furthermore, could we care for that child?

I made some tea and toast and headed to the sofa with a pen and notepad to figure out our dilemma. The early sun burst through the parted curtains and took the chill from the morning air. I sat in its path and stared at the blank notepad, which was made brighter yellow where the sun landed on it.

What did I know about abused children? Not too much; however, I remembered a distant cousin from many years prior. She was a single, teenaged mom who had given birth to a baby girl. At nineteen years old, she was already living by herself and working to support herself. The birth of her daughter was an unhappy event for her family, and it proved to be too much for her. One night after split shifts at the restaurant all week, the mom picked up the baby and took her home. The baby was sick with a fever and cried hysterically, but the mother didn't know what to do. Initially, she just left the baby in the crib. But after enduring hours of screaming, the exhausted, frustrated, and angry teenaged mom stomped to the crib, intending to force the stubborn baby to stop crying. She snatched up the baby and began shaking her. When she finished, the baby was quiet. But then, something else was wrong. The baby, barely breathing, was unresponsive.

The ambulance came and took her to the local hospital, where immediately the decision was made to transport the baby to Children's Hospital in Denver. As my mother was the only family living locally, she was asked to attend the baby at the hospital. When she arrived with us kids in tow, the baby had severe brain damage and swelling. It was unknown that day whether or not she would live.

The little girl proved to be a fighter, but social services took custody of her. She spent the rest of her childhood in foster homes, eventually moving to a group home when she was old enough, as she never fully developed mentally. She lives there to this day.

Ugh. That was my experience with abused infants. I suddenly felt sick. Maybe we should rethink adopting through foster care and reconsider private adoption. True, it would be more expensive, but at least we would know that the baby wasn't abused. We would take the baby home directly from the hospital and could be certain of his safety.

The truth was I didn't think I could care for a baby who had physical needs. I had some physical needs. I had chronic illness, and because of it, I spent my share of days feeling sick and weak. How could I care for a baby with physical needs when I was struggling myself?

Unfortunately, I didn't have to work that day, and therefore, I spent the day thinking, rethinking, and overthinking what special needs our baby might have if we adopted through foster care. The issue snowballed in my head as the day went on, and when John finally got home, he must have felt like he was hit with a fire hose.

I unloaded all my concerns on him. *Maybe we should go through private adoption.... Yes, it is expensive, but in the long run we would ensure ourselves a healthy baby. You can't put a price on that! Through foster care, we cannot be sure what has happened to the baby. Which path would lead us to our baby? The right baby for us?*

John listened patiently to my concerns, which were delivered in near-hysteria and simply replied, "God will bring the right baby—our baby—to us wherever we are."

While John's statement immediately reassured me, it also reminded me of some truths: 1) God would meet us where we were; 2) God would never give us more than we could handle without His help; and 3) My lack of faith was fully exposed.

I had just experienced a spiritual and emotional smackdown.

And it wouldn't be the last one on this journey.

Chapter 9
Food for Thought

Karen handed each couple a three-ring binder and began the first foster parent training class by explaining what happens when a child is taken into custody by social services. The child must be placed with a foster family, first and foremost. Based on parent history and present circumstances among other things, the caseworkers make an educated guess whether to place the child in a foster-to-adopt home or a traditional foster care home. Since this was a "legal risk" class, Karen spoke about the foster-to-adopt process.

As soon as their child has been taken into custody, the biological parents are required to appear before the judge within a week. If the judge affirms that the child is unsafe with his parents, a parenting plan is established and a visitation schedule is set. The parenting plan, which is not always revealed to the foster parents, may consist of random drug tests, parenting classes, counseling sessions, visits with their child, and other court appearances to name few. The judge also determines the number of hours and days the biological parents will visit with their child. The parents are considered successful if they complete about 70 percent of the parenting plan.

The couples in the room began to whisper among themselves at that statistic. It was unthinkable that a parent who only made it to seven out of ten visits with their child was considered successful; and furthermore, it was astonishing that an adult who had three out of ten "hot" drug tests was successful!

Karen must have sensed she dropped a bomb, because at that point she asked if anyone had questions.

One gentleman raised his hand and asked if the parents needed to find jobs as part of the parenting plan. No, not necessarily, she said, as the county had funds to help them with their food and housing.

The air was charged with judgment, and the room fell silent.

Many times, she explained, these parents have serious personal issues. They may have drug or alcohol addictions; they may be abusive or violent individuals; they may even have engaged in criminal activity. Often, their issues keep them from holding down a steady job. In fact, some of the same issues that keep them from a job are also keeping them from properly caring for their children. The parenting plan gives them a certain amount of time to get their lives together, or at least demonstrate that they are truly trying. Keep in mind, she continued, that Colorado Law states that foster children up to six years old must be placed in their permanent homes—be it an adoptive home or their biological home—within a year. The biological parents really don't have that much time to show they are trying to turn their lives around, and the judge is very strict with them. If they aren't showing motivation, he will terminate their parental rights sooner. Their immediate goal needs to be overcoming their personal issues for their children's sake. Their employment goals will come later.

She managed to defuse our judgment, which was her goal. As a caseworker, she saw both sides. She saw the pain of the parents who couldn't overcome their demons and, as a result, lost their children. She also saw the joy of the couples who for the first time would become parents. It was hard to take sides on an issue where someone lost everything so someone else could gain.

That tore at me. It was a lot easier to think about the biological parents as some kind of monsters instead of regular people struggling to overcome their bad choices and failing. *I mean, who hasn't made bad choices?*

Somehow I sensed these classes would be harder than I anticipated.

Chapter 10
Attachments

I would say that, in general, I am a happy person. Not the kind who dots my "i's" with hearts or anything like that. But I am drawn to novels with glorious endings, sunrises so fresh that owls can still be heard hooting, and all weddings and baptisms, which leave me in a puddle of tears, even if they happen in cartoons.

But I was beginning to dread the foster parent training classes. All the conversations were about abuse, neglect, and abandonment of children by their own parents and how the children were affected. Terrible things that one wouldn't wish on terrorists. I'm not exactly sure what I expected to hear at the classes, but the detail into which she delved blanketed me with such sadness that I had trouble shaking it for days.

Nonetheless, I went and pasted on my best fake smile, the one that I developed early on when my Mom would remind me that the earth didn't revolve around me and nobody was interested in hearing my problems. Among my sisters, the fake smile was also known as "perma-grin."

Anyway, Karen spoke that night on attachment. Everybody knew what normal attachment looked like, but what inhibits proper attachment and what is the result?

The most severe attachment issues were classified as Reactive Attachment Disorders (RAD). Those disorders were caused by ongoing neglect or abuse. Babies need to feel that their needs are being met when they communicate (cry). When they aren't fed, changed, or stimulated regularly by a familiar caregiver on an ongoing basis, then rejection, anger, and hopelessness sets in. Generally, these same babies don't get the cuddling, eye contact, and playtime they need either, so they give up expecting their needs to be met. They lose the trust and security that are essential to proper attachment, and down the road they develop social misbehaviors. Often, she continued, children who suffer from RAD have come from orphanages, where there are different caregivers caring for a dozen or more babies at once. In that situation, it is just impossible to give each baby the attention he needs. Rarely does RAD happen to the children in foster care, she claimed, because the county tries to minimize the number of times a child goes to a new placement and the number of children per household. Therefore, the county tries to ensure that the child has consistent care by the fewest number of caregivers possible.

She passed out sheets of paper with circle diagrams and flow charts, and that's when she lost me. *I couldn't read diagrams and flow charts! I was a liberal arts major! I couldn't even read a map! And furthermore, I'd rather stay home than try!* Those charts and diagrams were an engineer's dream! I looked over at my husband, an engineer by profession, and thought for a moment that his eyes danced with enthusiasm. He was examining those charts like a cheetah hunting a gazelle. He might have been salivating for all I knew.

I trusted that he could hit the highlights for me later, and I let my mind wander back to a nonverbal communications class I took in college. I vaguely remembered reading a study about some orphanages in Germany in the 1940s. Maybe it was Romania. Anyway, those babies were the children of unwed mothers or mothers too poor to care for them. They were taken to the orphanages where the babies were fed regularly from bottles that had been propped up for them. Their diapers were regularly changed, and they were kept clean and safe. However, they were rarely held, cuddled, or engaged because the workers reasoned that the babies would bond better with their adoptive parents if they didn't already have attachments. They were wrong. The study showed that at one orphanage, one-third of the babies died. And that was the low end. At the high end in more than one orphanage, 90 percent of the babies died. Their findings were that babies can be fed, sheltered, and kept warm and clean, but without being held, cuddled, touched, and loved, they have an abnormal tendency to die. To me, the attachment disorders felt like one step short of that abysmal death by isolation. They both had the same characteristics: loss, grief, rejection, and lack of touch, attention, and interaction.

When I turned my attention back to Karen, she was explaining that RAD was the most severe attachment disorder, but there was a spectrum of attachment issues to be aware of. Adopted children were particularly susceptible to attachment issues as they have already experienced loss, grief, and rejection. And attachment wasn't only an infant issue. Those problems could pop up at any point in their lives.

It was a fascinating thing to be studying attachment issues in a classroom with the benefit of time and distance. It was a scary thing to be studying it at a training class because it could become your reality. How would I recognize the symptoms? How would I fix it? Were there follow-up classes for attachment disorders or was a psychologist consulted?

The classes were stirring up more questions than they answered, and that night as we left I couldn't even muster my best perma-grin.

Chapter 11

A Flicker of Hope

A little pep talk was needed before I dragged myself to the night's foster parent training class. On the way, a strange thought flashed in my mind. A little valium might go a long way to ease the anxiety the classes caused. It was a strange thought—and a little ironic—because some of the children were in foster care because their parents indulged in recreational drugs. *Where did these thoughts come from?*

I was losing my mind, plain and simple.

We arrived and learned that the topics for the night were Drugs and Alcohol. *Perfect.* Something to look forward to. I braced myself for the oncoming emotional slaughter.

Karen began by explaining the effects of marijuana on

children in utero. Marijuana was extremely carcinogenic; it had hundreds of chemicals that crossed the placenta and affected the baby. It could be found in the baby's body up to a month after a single use. Furthermore, marijuana caused the fetus to get less food and oxygen, and therefore, affected the baby's growth and brain development. Babies exposed to marijuana could likely develop learning delays and attention disorders.

Cocaine was another issue for some of the babies taken into protective custody. Also able to cross the placenta, cocaine stimulated the baby far longer than the mother stayed stimulated. Babies born to cocaine users were often easily startled by loud noises, which resulted in ongoing screaming fits. Many of these children developed an array of cognitive delays that would likely resolve themselves with therapy around the age of two.

Meth was a fairly new drug. It was unknown what, if any, effects it may have on babies in utero. It hadn't been around long enough, at the time, to study its effects.

And that, along with alcohol, was how they defined "abused" newborn babies. Oddly, I was relieved. I expected to hear that drug-exposed babies were born without organs or limbs, and sometimes they were, but Karen said the majority of them just had physical or cognitive delays, which usually resolved around two to three years of age.

I could handle that! Suddenly, I was ecstatic! I could take my baby to physical therapy or speech therapy or feeding therapy or whatever. I didn't have a problem with that! Knowing that at some point, he would catch up with other children his age made my heart soar! Finally, there was a type of abused child that I thought I could parent! I wanted to jump up and dance and yell, "I'm not totally incompetent!"

As a child, I had a sister with a speech issue. I understood her just fine. Maybe that was my gift? *Children with delays, not disabilities?* My sister spent years in speech therapy and she grew out of it eventually and these kids would too! There was hope for me! I could adopt! Knowing that, I was on cloud nine. We took a short break and then reconvened for the second half of the class.

Full of confidence, I was eager to hear what was coming next. But what came next left me wanting to quit altogether....

Chapter 12
Hitting Rock Bottom

After the break, Karen was going to address the effects of alcohol in utero.

She began by saying that while drug-exposed infants caught up developmentally by their toddler years, alcohol-exposed infants, in contrast, were permanently impaired. The extent and severity of the damage depended on how much and at what points of development the mother drank. Alcohol uniquely crossed the blood-brain barrier and caused physical damage to the developing brain. The most severe cases were called Fetal Alcohol Syndrome, where there were facial deformities and the size of the brain was smaller than normal. The synapses in the brain often failed to trigger, causing communication problems between the left and right brain. Less severe cases were on the Fetal Alcohol Spectrum and may include anything from cognitive issues, like processing facts and attempting to recall them, to social communication cues or attention disorders to motor skills.

Suddenly, my heart was heavy for those children and their parents. I had a niece with dyslexia. She would study her spelling words every night of the week. She may have done them perfectly half a dozen times, but the day of the test, it was anybody's guess what might happen. Her recall abilities were impaired. To be diagnosed with Fetal Alcohol Spectrum Disorder (FASD), a child had to have a few of the typical alcohol-affected issues. So, for example, the child might have learning disabilities, attention disorders, and speech-language issues as well as neurological problems.

I couldn't imagine trying to parent a child with so many issues. The frustration with their challenges was one issue, but the child's perception of himself and his struggles to be like other children must just crush the hearts of his parents—not to mention how cruel other children can be when someone is a little different. The mama bear in me would be in full-on attack mode at all times. I would just be waiting for someone to make an off comment, so I could devour them. I could often be defensive, but to protect my FASD child, I would be a nut job incarnate. The mere thought of that drained my energy, and I turned my attention back to Karen.

She was saying that birth mothers will go to great lengths to hide the fact that they drank alcohol during their pregnancy. For one, they are embarrassed that they exposed their child to alcohol and fear the judgment upon themselves, but for two, they know that of all the "abuses" of a newborn baby, alcohol is the most severe and the least wanted by adoptive parents. She will lie about drinking because she wants her child placed in a "good" home, but too often adoptive parents don't want to take on children with these issues. *To be honest, I didn't want a child with Fetal Alcohol Syndrome or FASD! That would be a game-changer for me.*

"You need to know, if a woman has exposed her child to drugs in utero, there is a 99 percent chance that she has exposed him to alcohol as well," Karen said directly.

What I heard was: *all newborn babies placed for adoption through the county had Fetal Alcohol Syndrome or Spectrum Disorder, and therefore, would have lifelong disabilities.* I trembled with a sadness that radiated from my core. My heart began to beat wildly and I found it difficult to breathe. Adopting a baby through the county meant taking on a baby who had some degree of brain damage.

It was too much for me. I was heartbroken.

I managed to hold back the sobs until we reached the car. Then, through a flood of stinging tears, I told John it was time to quit.

Chapter 13
An Intervention of Sorts

My Dad had died two years earlier. He had battled esophageal cancer for nearly a year at that point. I remember when he knew he was dying.

I had arrived at his house mid-morning on a Tuesday to find his pastor and several elders around the hospital bed that was set up for him in the family room.

"What's going on?" I asked, looking around the room.

"I had a visit from the death angel last night," my Dad said calmly.

I slipped into a chair beside his bed, stunned at his statement. I didn't know how to process that. This was my Dad, the man who took me to Sunday school and taught me about Jesus. This was the man who allowed me as a child to climb up and recline on his Santa-sized belly and watch TV. We took nightly walks together when I was a teenager, and he quizzed me on my biology tests in school, sometimes until two in the morning when he had to get up at six. He was my date to countless Christian music concerts, attended all my softball games, and beamed the brightest when I graduated from college. He practiced his waltz over and over again, so he would make me proud at my wedding. *He was my dad! Where was his healing?*

I always thought we'd have more time. He adored my husband, and I imagined that once we were married, John and I and Mom and Dad would hang out and have dinners and games of Scrabble. I would get to know him better as an adult.

But just weeks after my wedding, he was diagnosed with cancer. His sickness took its toll on him, and the stress of the situation took a physical toll on my chronically ill body, not to mention my job and my fledgling marriage.

The elders from the church prayed over my dad and one by one said good-bye, each promising to see him later that week or the next. When they left, I pulled my chair directly in front of my Dad, leaned over to hug him, and asked over his shoulder, "Are you scared?" The tears escaped from my eyes and fell on his shirt.

"No," he assured me. "No, I'm not." He hugged me tight.

"I want to go too," I said, feeling sorry for myself. I was struggling physically, my marriage was brand new, I quit my job, and my Dad was about to be taken from me. I wanted it all to be over.

Dad grabbed my shoulders with a strength I didn't know he had left and said sternly, "No! It is not your time. You have not helped enough people. And I don't want to hear you say that again." He meant it too. He had a servant's heart. He wasn't considered "cool," neither was he welcomed in the "in" crowds, but he would stay late and vacuum the church, take out the trash, and mow the lawn on Saturdays when nobody else would. If someone needed a ride to church, he called Dad. And Dad was always available to help out when someone's car needed a jump-start. "Remember," he repeated, "you have not helped enough people." Thoroughly reprimanded, I didn't mention it again.

Three weeks later, he died.

Sometimes, people have seen their lost loved ones in their dreams, but that had not happened to me.

That is, until the night I wanted to quit the foster parent training classes.

In my dream, I was leaving a school of some sort. Floods of people were headed to the parking lot to go home, but at the end of the sidewalk, I saw Dad. He was walking against the crowd. He looked beautiful, healthy, and happy, and he was coming toward me. I stopped and waited. It was sunny and warm in my dream, and my dad was approaching me with a huge smile. I started to cry as he held out his arms to hug me.

"Do you remember?" he asked. "Do you?"

I nodded, unable to speak through my tears. It was so comforting to be held by my Dad, like I had been healed of an affliction I didn't know I had. I was restored.

I don't know how long he hugged me, but when he let go, he whispered, "I love you." Then he smiled, kissed my forehead, and walked away. Down the sidewalk, he disappeared.

I awakened with tears spilling onto my pillow, feeling happy and sad all at once.

I think I knew he wouldn't visit me again. I would have to be the one to go there. But, for now, I had work to do. I would not quit the foster parent training today.

Chapter 14
Another Dose of Doubt

When I was a kid, Mom would choose one day every summer to take my sisters and me downtown. She had lived downtown at the YWCA when she first came to America from Ireland and fully understood the magic and mystery of our capitol city. Or maybe she was just sentimental for it. In any case, it wasn't just any day; she made it into an event, one of the traditions I looked forward to every summer.

She would drive us down to Sloane's Lake, where we would catch the bus into the city. She didn't demand that we stay close either. We could sit wherever we wanted, which made me feel so independent. Of course, if the bus was full and an adult—or heaven forbid, an elderly person—got on the bus, we children were the first to give up our seats. *I mean, we were on holiday from the monotony of everyday life, not from our manners!* No matter, though, it was even more daring to ride the bus while we stood and held the metal rod.

Once downtown, we would shop. Nothing serious, of course. It was more like window shopping, but the point was to walk around and see the city. This was before 16th Street Mall was developed and became a huge draw. We always went to Penney's, May D&F (they had wonderful window displays), and Woolworth's. Ah, Woolworth's!

Once we got there, I'd look around for the café. It was separated from the store, but had cut-out windows in the walls where you could see people eating. On the perimeter of the diner, the booths were upholstered with shiny, red vinyl. A long counter, which sat directly in the middle of the restaurant, was raised slightly higher than the tables and was bordered with red vinyl-upholstered bar stools. And everything, everything was trimmed with chrome from the laminated tabletops and countertop to the bar stools and wall behind the counter. Polished to a sparkle, it looked like the summer version of Christmas tinsel. The food had to be good in a diner that looked like that! I now know what draws men to classic cars. It's the chrome. A man's version of diamonds.

Only once did we eat at the counter, but that didn't matter. Each of us got our own menu and was allowed to order anything we wanted. I felt so grown up. Cheeseburgers and fries were the features of the menu, but to us, it felt like filet mignon. We'd savor each bite, because when the meal was over, it was time to find the bus and head home. We wouldn't come back again until the following summer.

I loved that trip downtown. It was one of my favorite traditions. My family had dozens of traditions.

"And we can make our own," which is what I told John when he was wavering on adopting after a foster training class on loss. Karen had talked about all the things adoptive children were losing when they lost their birth parents. Among them were traditions, birth order, siblings, ancestry, and culture. He felt that our child would be losing too much that was insurmountable.

One by one we went through the list. Traditions: we'd make our own, not better or worse, just different. Birth order: well, our child would be adopted by somebody and his birth order wouldn't necessarily be what it would have been in his biological family anyway. Why should that be an obstacle for us? Siblings: he'd have other adopted siblings and, as with ancestry, we'd promise our children that we would help them find their birth family when they attained the age of majority, if they chose. Finally, culture: our schools had become so diverse that helping him learn about his culture, whatever that may be, might be an enjoyable adventure.

Our family wouldn't be perfect, I argued. None are.

"Before we quit," I suggested, "let's just go to the last class. Please." I couldn't believe that I was the one talking John out of his tree this time. Just the week before, I wanted to quit.

Anyway, we had only one class left. It was the panel and I was anxious to see some of the children adopted through foster care and hear their stories. It was one thing to hear stories from Karen, it was another to hear from the parents who had been through it.

Chapter 15
The Last Class

The day I had been looking forward to had arrived. We were going to meet three adoptive parents who had taken this journey before us, and we were instructed to ask any questions we wanted when they finished sharing their stories.

Three women sat at the head of the room, waiting to be introduced. Two of them had children on their laps, one a girl and one a boy. The other must have been the adoptive mother to the two teenaged girls who sat to the side of the room, all shy and giggling among themselves. Karen stood and introduced each lady and picked the mother with the little girl on her lap to begin.

I was so anxious to hear their stories that my heart was beating like a wildebeest. *Why was I getting nervous?* I sat on the edge of my chair, balancing my weight over my elbows on the table, as if somehow I was privy to a delicious secret.

The mom had sandy brown, shoulder-length hair several shades darker than the little girl on her lap. As she spoke, she wrestled with the active little girl to keep her seated. They were placed with the little girl, Emma, when she was a newborn, shortly after their first disruption. Emma had been born to a woman who was addicted to meth, and although the birth mother regularly attended visits with the child, her parental rights were terminated after eight months because her drug tests continued to be "hot."

The woman described how Emma was a "screamer" as a baby, probably due to the drugs in utero, she had speech delays still and was always hyperactive. As if to punctuate that point, Emma popped off her mother's lap and began to run around the room, darting under tables and slithering under chairs. At one point, she stepped onto a square of unoccupied carpet and began to dance and spin and hum to herself, all the while watching her floaty, summer dress twist and twirl around her legs.

Mother #2, who I thought was probably barely forty herself, described how she adopted her grandson after her daughter fell in with a bad crowd and also became addicted to drugs. She was asked how that situation worked when she still had contact with her daughter. Ultimately, she explained, she was the guardian. She did allow her daughter to visit, but she was the one responsible for the sweet little two-year-old boy. It seemed to me that she had a tough time of it. She had raised her daughter and now, single, was about to raise her grandson as well.

And Mother #3 adopted the two sisters after she and her husband had already raised six biological children themselves. *Six?* I tried to picture myself with six children, but my mind wouldn't allow me to go there. Even if I could imagine it, I didn't think I would add two more when the others flew the coop. It was more likely that I'd lock up the house, disconnect the phone, and sleep for six months. God bless the couple who would open their hearts and home to two school-aged orphans, who might otherwise not have been adopted or allowed to stay together.

All the way home, John and I discussed the stories of the women on the panel. And while we agreed that each situation was amazing, we related most closely with Emma's mother, a woman who built her family through adoption. As we recounted the parts of her story that struck each of us, I remembered that she had glazed over a certain detail. She had fleetingly mentioned their "first disruption." I had been too charmed by Emma's antics to pay close attention to her mother's words. It was only after I got home that I heard what she said. And now, it was too late to ask. *What happened with their first disruption?*

Chapter 16
Caught Off Guard

One month after the foster parent training classes ended, John and I still hadn't submitted our applications. To be precise, we hadn't even opened the envelope. I was sure that we would adopt through the county, but the classes had drained us, and it was just too soon for us to press on. It was similar to a boxer who has taken a blow to the head and needs to steady himself before he reengages. That's where we were.

One Monday after work, I came home to a voice message from a county caseworker. She was just calling to follow up after the training classes, she said, and to see if we had any questions or needed help with the application. What I heard was, *"What's taking so long with your application?"*

I grabbed the thick brown envelope and slid its contents out onto the kitchen table. There were two identical applications, one for each of us to fill out. Each was about twenty-five pages and asked questions about me that I hadn't even contemplated. No multiple choice here. All essay. I set those aside.

Among what was left were three reference packets, not to be filled out by family members, of course, lest crazy vouch for crazy. Instructions for fingerprinting and photos and forms for physicals were also included. I picked up the form we were supposed to give to our physician and felt my heart quicken. One of the questions the county wanted answered was "Is so-and-so physically capable of caring for a child?" Well, I thought so, but what did my doctor think? I had been chronically ill since I was thirteen years old. I had never been in remission. She had treated me for twelve years and knew all about my physical limitations and issues. She had admitted me to the hospital several times over those years; she listened to me complain about how college was physically exhausting for me; and she knew how inconsistent I had been with my medication. What would she say?

The other question that worried me was "Does so-and-so have a normal life expectancy?" *Did I?* I had never thought about that until now. Does chronic illness lower one's life expectancy? And if so, by how much? I wasn't sure I wanted to know the answer to that one. And if I didn't have a normal life expectancy, did that mean I was ineligible to adopt?

The county included an addressed, postage-paid envelope with the physical form, so my doctor could send it directly to the county and her comments would be completely confidential. Just my luck.

Control freak that I was, I decided I couldn't just leave this to chance. I already had my physical for the year, but John hadn't. I would make his appointment and at the end of his physical, I would present her with the paperwork and state my case. I planned to make it clear that I was capable of caring for a child, and perhaps more difficult, state all the ways I planned to be healthier in the future. Thus, extending my life expectancy. *Is that even possible?*

Hmmm, I would have to give this whole thing some serious thought. I didn't want to give her a reason to add "mental illness" to her physician's report.

Chapter 17
Making Mountains out of Molehills

The day of John's physical had arrived. When I made the appointment, I made sure it would be okay for me to join John and Dr. Katherine at the end. I wanted to discuss the paperwork we needed her to fill out for our foster parent certification.

I started seeing Dr. Katherine twelve years earlier after my first physical had been performed by a male doctor. Suffice it to say, I was scarred for life. That was the first and last physical that a male doctor was doing on me! I knew me and I knew I wouldn't go again if a man had to do it. I was seeing other male specialists for various reasons, so I started polling their nurses about who they thought was the best female general practitioner. Three different nurses recommended Dr. Katherine and that's when I made the switch. I loved her and had been with her ever since. Then, when we married, John started seeing her as well.

Getting John to this year's physical was easier than most years, because it was linked to a purpose. Most years, I would make the appointment and John would reschedule it at least once. He argued that since nothing was wrong, he really didn't need to go. I suspected he didn't like seeing a female practitioner, but since he never went to the doctor, it was just easy to go to her. To be fair, I fully understood his trepidation, but I pretended that he was overreacting. If I sympathized with him, he might not go at all. It was a tough love thing.

While he was in with Dr. Katherine, I sat in the waiting room rehearsing my speech in my head. There were two questions on the physician's report that I wanted to address with her. Actually, I wanted to preempt her from writing something about my health that would negate our adoption.

From a physician's point of view, was I (as someone with chronic illness) expected to live a normal life expectancy? I didn't know the answer to that, and I didn't know if I wanted to. So, I decided to argue that I wasn't even thirty years old yet. If we were placed with a baby in the next year, he would be eighteen years old before I was fifty. Surely, I was expected to live to fifty years old! Even my mother, who had her own health challenges, was alive and well into her fifties now. Regardless of my life expectancy, I was still young enough to raise a child into adulthood. *Right?*

Again, from a physician's point of view, was I capable of caring for a child? Again, I thought so. But even when I had flare-ups, I had a wonderful support system. My mom and two sisters were anxious to help, and I had several friends who already claimed babysitting rights when we were placed with a baby. That's not even to mention how helpful John was. He could take time off when I was in the hospital. So, in my head, I rehearsed every answer to every question I could imagine she might ask.

Dr. Katherine and John finished up, and I was called back into the exam room. I handed Dr. Katherine the paperwork and explained that we needed them for our certification. She briefly looked the papers over and excused herself to get my chart. While she was gone, I glanced at John. He looked slightly green, and I asked him if he was feeling unwell.

"I've just been violated," he responded, somewhat dramatically, I thought.

Oh, here we go! I rolled my eyes. There was no point engaging in this conversation. The drama might get worse.

Dr. Katherine reentered the room, reading the paperwork more closely this time. I saw her brows furrow, and I thought I might need oxygen. She turned slowly and closed the door behind her. She continued reading as she crossed the room and took her chair. A lone pen abandoned on the counter was snatched up, and she began to scribble notes. I looked around for an air sickness bag. What were they called when you weren't on an airplane? *Sickness bags?*

Silence still. *What could she possibly be noting?*

This woman had the power to affect our adoption, and I had just aged a decade in her presence. Uncomfortable with the silence, I was about to launch into my monologue. But suddenly, she announced that everything looked good to her. Glancing back at the paperwork, she began to nod. Yes, she said, she thought we would make excellent parents!

And that was it! No salesmanship needed. No defending my illness or my support system or my life expectancy. I knew better than to proceed anyway. I didn't want to bring up issues she may not have thought about.

We thanked her and left immediately. And I was ready to go off and make my next mountain out of a molehill.

Chapter 18
Mission Accomplished

Application submitted, we applied ourselves to completing the rest of the to-do list for the county. References from friends who would say that the sun rose at our mere request? Check. CPR taught by an instructor who resembled Barney Fife but had none of his fun, nervous ticks? This man was tall and lanky, all limbs and clumsiness. His cowboy boots served as anchors on his feet, and he walked mechanically like the Tin Man from *The Wizard of Oz.* When he spoke, he stretched out each syllable in a dry, monotone manner, but not in a charming, Southern-accent kind of way. I wasn't sure I'd be able to stay awake for the eight hours to complete that one. Check. Fingerprints? Mine were so worn down that the officer told me to stop doing dishes for a week and then come back and try again. *Right then and there, she became my new best friend.* Check. And finally, financial statements. It sounded simple enough, but the county was looking for more than our W-2s. They wanted our tax returns for a couple of years, credit reports, and outstanding debts and pay-off dates in order to insure our solvency. I mean, they didn't want to rescue us and our adopted children from a cardboard box down by the Platte River. That would certainly make the evening news. Financial statements? Check.

Well, the county was nothing if not thorough. They touched on everything but my weight. And I meant the real one, not the one on my driver's license, which they already had. All that was left was our psychological evaluation.

When the psychologist called to schedule the appointment, she indicated that it would take six hours. *Six hours?!?!* Two with John and me together, two by myself, and two with John by himself.

We spent the morning scouring the house from attic to basement in case she wanted a tour. My mom always said that you never get a second chance at a first impression, so don't embarrass the family. In her mind, you were never an individual or by extension, isolated. You were part of a unit, the family, and everything you said or did reflected back on "the family." On the flip side, though, "the family" always had your back, like a small army waiting to do battle. I was struck by how much her words influenced me. I heard her voice in my head, complete with Irish brogue, and I wondered if someday I would have the same influence on my children. *Did all mothers have influence over their children like that, or was my mother particularly strong?*

House sparkling, I had an hour to pass before the psychologist arrived. I positively trembled from anxiety and wondered how I could prepare for this evaluation. I was a planner. I prepared, plotted, and planned for just about everything I did. I cursed spontaneity, and I loathed that I didn't know what to expect from the evaluation either. Either I was crazy or I was not! That was the bottom line. I didn't think I was, but you don't know what you don't know. I once heard a man say, "Pigs don't know pigs stink!" If you are a pig, you don't know you stink. Likewise, if you are crazy, you don't know you're short on marbles!

The psychologist arrived, accepted refreshments, and settled into the oversized chair by the window. As she took out her notebook, she casually mentioned that her daughter had the same chronic illness that I had. She told me her daughter's amazing story and asked me about mine and it was like two old friends had been catching up on lost years. We exchanged tips and recommendations between questions, and the hours slipped by without my noticing. As I looked back on that evaluation, I believed it was a little gift from God.

And I knew we had achieved our certification.

Chapter 19
The First
Support Group

Our caseworker from the county called to congratulate us on our foster parent certification even before we officially received our certificate in the mail. She also invited us to attend the foster-to-adopt support group which met on the first Thursday of every month, if we chose. This coming Thursday as a matter of fact. *Hmm. Membership had its privileges.*

However, she reminded me, if we didn't choose to attend, we needed to be accruing twenty hours of training credits to renew our certification each year. We might have to pay out-of-pocket for them if we took classes outside Adams County. The support groups counted as two training hours each, and they were free to county foster parents. Just something to keep in mind, she said. *Okay, then. They were highly encouraged.*

There was a discrepancy between the reality of the support group and my expectations. When the caseworker said "support group," I imagined a roomful of foster parents sharing their stories, airing their grievances, and gathering advice from others who were farther along on the journey. I thought that the foster parents probably exchanged phone numbers and relied on one another to sustain them emotionally between court appearances. And I was anxious to listen and learn from their wisdom and experiences.

Instead, the county invited a speaker. His name was Carl and he introduced himself as the county attorney. He announced that he would be explaining the judicial process in regards to foster children, and at the end he would take questions. However, he wouldn't address specific questions about individual cases, so please make sure they only related to the judicial process. We had just covered this in our initial "boot camp" training, as I was sure everyone else had in theirs, so the class seemed redundant to me. But I guess if they were offering training hours for the support group, there needed to be some training going on.

I looked around the room and spotted an infant car seat on the floor. I grabbed a pen and paper and scribbled a quick note to John, who was sitting right beside me:

That couple has a baby. Car seat is under the table. Let's go over and talk to them afterward.

John nodded his consent, and I did my best to focus on the rest of the lecture. Carl finally finished up but left only fifteen minutes to answer questions.

The first question came from a woman in the back. "Who do I need to notify when I plan an intervention?"

Intervention? What was an intervention? We didn't learn about that in "boot camp."

The question set Carl on edge. "Your caseworker," he snapped. "For those of you who don't know: an intervention is the right of the foster parents who have had the child in their home at least three months to show up and testify in court. But we highly discourage it. It muddies the waters. You see, sometimes we are pursuing an adoption plan and a reunification plan at the same time. If the foster parents show up, the biological parents think we have been pursuing adoption all along. The biological parents then argue that they haven't had a fair shake because the county was pursuing adoption all along."

Huh? Didn't we think they were pursuing adoption all along? That's why it's called foster-to-adopt.

Nobody offered a follow up question, so Carl continued, "We are pursuing what is best for the child. Just trust us to do our jobs. We will tell you what happened in court."

Carl wrapped things up, and John and I raced over to the couple with the baby. We introduced ourselves, as did they, and I asked to meet their baby. Tom lifted the car seat to the table and Gloria pulled back the blankets. Underneath was a sweet little boy with a thick shock of black hair, whose sleep was being disturbed by the fluorescent lights. He squinted and wiggled and kicked in his sleep. Gloria said he was eight-weeks-old and had been born to a mother who used meth. She only showed up for some of her scheduled visits with him and still had "hot" drug tests, so it appeared likely that he would be adopted. Tom and Gloria had him since birth.

I congratulated them and asked what the baby's name was. Gloria shot the caseworkers and Carl a look and simply said, "His birth parents named him David." We had been encouraged in our "boot camp" classes to keep the child's biological name. It is his original identity and it served as a link to his birth family. But I had the impression that Tom and Gloria planned to name him something else. Again, I congratulated them on a beautiful baby and wished them good luck.

We left and I recapped the week's events in my mind. 1) We were "invited" to support group, but it was strongly recommended, if not mandatory. 2) Support group was not intended to encourage interpersonal connection between foster parents, but rather used by the county as continuing education. 3) The county "discouraged" intervention. Just don't do it as it will ultimately threaten your adoption. 4) Foster parents fully intended to change their child's birth name as soon as they adopted him, against the advice of the county.

We had only been certified for six days and I was beginning to see a pattern. The pattern was that many things at the county were understood, but not expressed. I hated games like this. For one, they made me feel like the dumb girl. *How could I not know?*

But for two, when it comes to our placement, what should I know that I am not being told?

Chapter 20
Are We There Yet?

Most every July, Mom would get an itch to go on a weekend getaway. July meant that the destination would be Frontier Days. Mom and Dad would wake us very early on Saturday morning and throw our pillows and blankets into the back of the station wagon, so we could finish sleeping on the way up. Then, we would set off on our hundred-mile excursion to meet Grandma and Grandpa at the Eagle's Club for the Frontier Days' Pancake Breakfast hosted there.

For the most part, we slept the majority of the way up. However, there were occasions when once up, we stayed up. On those occasions, Dad, who was an engineer for the state's department of transportation, would explain to us how the city was planned on a grid: in general, streets that ran East and West were "avenues," while streets that ran North and South were "streets," with the exception of state highways. Additionally, the plan was for the streets to be marked alphabetically and the avenues would be marked numerically. Then, we would take turns reading the street names out loud. Hey, when you say you're bored, your parents will find something to occupy you, and I guess you teach your children what you know. Right? Eventually, we learned to make it a competition. Who could shout out the name of the next street first? To this day, I can be dropped anywhere in the middle of that city and find my way home. A foreign language might have been more serviceable, but you take what you get. Right? Anyway, once out of the city and heading north on the highway, boredom set in once again. I mean, there are only so many unique bridges and ramps on this long stretch of road. Somewhere a few miles down the highway, we would begin to ask, "Are we there yet?" The answer was always "No," of course. But mere minutes later, we would ask again in our most pained voices. Are we there yet? Are we there yet? *Are we there YET?* The wait was killing us!

When John and I finished our foster parent certification, I called Karen every week to remind her that we were waiting. What I wanted to say was, "Karen, this is Julie. John and I are ready to take the very next baby you have available, even if it's half-alien and was hatched in the parking lot. We can be reached twenty-four hours a day. Here is our home phone, John's cell phone, my cell phone, and my mother's home phone. We have been waiting for three weeks! Please call ASAP!" But that sounded a little desperate. So instead I left messages that said, "Hi, Karen, this is Julie. I just wanted to remind you that we are available when you have a foster-to-adopt baby to place. Hope you have a great week! Bye-bye." I used my best I'm-just-casually-waiting-and-remembered-out-of-the-blue-to-call-you voice. But I marked it on our calendar: "Monday, 10 a.m., call Karen." Not that I needed to. It was all I thought about. I felt like a child who had been promised a puppy, but hadn't gotten it yet. I positively shook with anticipation.

Eventually, she returned my call, telling me that a reminder every second or third week would be fine, especially since it was the holidays. That was code for "remember, we try not to place children over the holidays." It was true and we had been told that if at all possible, the county avoided placing children in permanent homes at the beginning of the school year and at Thanksgiving/Christmas. Adoptive parents wanted their child to start school with the rest of the children and sometimes took whatever placement was offered, even if they thought it might not be a good fit for them. That rushed decision sometimes resulted in the child returning to social services because of unacceptable behaviors that weren't carefully considered.

The same was true at Thanksgiving and Christmas. Adoptive parents wanted to be placed immediately, so they could shower their new child with presents and introduce them to extended family. Often, the adoptive parents ignored warnings that made the placement ultimately fail.

We were told all about that. We simply finished our certification at an unfortunate time and would have to wait a little longer to be placed. Until then, though, I would keep leaving messages for Karen and I would think up something to do with myself.

In fact, I already knew exactly what I would do....

Chapter 21
Begin with the End in Mind

Hi. My name is Julie and I am a nerd.

And by nerd, I mean that if there is a precise formula to achieve my goals, I will follow it to the letter. For example, as a student, I wanted to have the best grades. I didn't want the best grades I could get, I wanted the best grades. Period. I came home from school every day, grabbed a snack, and immediately sat down at the dining room table to begin what could be six hours of homework. And that was just junior high school. If the teachers said "read this" or "do that," I did. And it worked. My freshman year in high school, I was ranked #1 out of 600 students. My sophomore year, I began dating and my goals changed, … but that is a story for another time.

So, I am a nerd and I married an engineer, which is basically the same thing. *(This begs the joke, "What do engineers use for birth control? Their personalities.")* Anyway, we were a couple waiting to be placed with a baby, over the holidays, and I was anxious to do something while we waited. During that time, John was an avid Stephen R. Covey fan, and though I didn't read his book *The Seven Habits of Highly Successful People*, I knew from John that Mr. Covey advocated beginning with the end in mind.

That gave me an idea.

I set out to find pictures of the most beautiful babies I could find. I figured that since they wouldn't look like us anyway, I would pick the ones I thought were most beautiful to visualize my goals. For the next two weeks, I collected magazines from doctors' offices, perused magazines at the library, and bought magazines from the bookstore. Everywhere I went, I flipped through magazines. And not just parenting magazines. I thumbed through every magazine I came across just in case there was an advertisement with a picture of a baby.

John and I both came from families with three children, so we thought three a good number. Ecclesiastes 4:12 states, "A cord of three strands is not quickly broken." However, as I was choosing the pictures, I remembered my baby sister saying she felt left out sometimes when we played as children. Maybe with four children, they could pair off and each have a playmate. Like the animals on Noah's ark, each was half of a pair. I was beginning to overthink the exercise, as usual, so I settled on four pictures. God could sort it out.

I cut out one picture of a beautiful baby boy, maybe two or three months old, with red hair and cornflower blue eyes. He was lying on a cobalt blue blanket. Another picture was of a newborn baby with near-black eyes and dark hair. That baby's gender wasn't apparent. The third baby was a little girl with brown eyes and dark hair on a pink and white gingham blanket. And finally, the last baby was toddler-aged with gorgeous blue eyes, a huge smile, and fat rolls on his legs. Best of all, besides being beautiful, they all looked happy. That was also important to me.

I took it one step further. Truly, as far as visualizing my goals, I went way off the deep end. I enlisted John's help in making a list of characteristics we would like our child to have. "Nice laugh," "honest," "loves Jesus," "kind," and "good teeth" were all attributes we added to the page of yellow legal paper that we filled on both sides. Since I was setting goals, I wanted to be specific.

I stuck all of it, four pictures and the list of characteristics, to the refrigerator with magnets. Then, I would be reminded of my goals every time I touched the door, which was often because when I was anxious, I ate. Hello, my name is Julie and I also nibble when I'm anxious.

Content that we had all details addressed, John and I prayed over our goals. We were giddy with anticipation and optimistic about the baby that we would adopt. I mean, with specific goals and fervent prayer, how can you go wrong?

Chapter 22
Cracking the Code

About a week into the New Year, I received a peculiar e-mail from the county that read: "Would you take a Hispanic baby?" It was strange to me because we were required to fill out a "characteristics form" as part of our application. The form detailed many characteristics that foster care children may have. It included all races as well as many diseases and deformities such as Fetal Alcohol Syndrome, HIV/AIDS, Hydrocephalus, club foot, etc. We were asked to check the situations we thought we could handle.

As I have said before, I know couples who only wanted children of their own race, regardless of their physical limitations. Some couples only wanted specific genders and the county worked with that as well. The caseworkers made it very clear that the more specific the demands, the longer the couple would wait to be placed. For example, if you said you only wanted a newborn, healthy, Caucasian baby girl, you might wait months if not over a year. If you were open to being placed with either gender of any race, you would likely be placed more quickly. That was the case with John and me. We had decided that our limitations, mine actually, were physical. Having a chronic illness meant that I had some physically limiting days. Therefore, having to care for a physically limited baby would be something I didn't think I could do on top of my own issues. Our request was for a healthy newborn baby, and we didn't set limits on race or gender, which is why the e-mail took me aback.

"Would you take a Hispanic baby?" *What did that mean? Didn't we already answer that question?* Immediately, my suspicious mind began searching for hidden meaning: *Do they think we shouldn't? Do they think we are unqualified to raise a transracially adopted child? Do they have a specific baby in mind? What are they really getting at? Was this a test?*

The e-mail came from a female caseworker. And as someone who has experience with women and is one herself, I could tell you that some women don't always say what they mean. For example, when we were teenagers getting ready for church on Sunday, my Mom would often ask, "Are you wearing that?" The question was loaded, of course, because she wasn't really looking for a simple yes or no. She was trying to say, "Choose something else. You look awful and you're going to embarrass yourself." Likewise, every man on the planet knows when his lady says to him, "Does this make me look fat?" we are not really asking if the outfit is flattering. (Be careful here, men!) Rather, we are seeking reassurance that we are still attractive to him.

I raced from the room to get John. His reaction was the same as mine, "What does that mean?"

"I don't know, but maybe there is something we are overlooking. For example, will the child resent being raised by Caucasian parents instead of Hispanic parents? Will we be able to adequately expose him to his culture and customs? Oh, and what about this: Will the difference in our skin color make him feel self-conscious and different from his peers?" I was beginning to worry. I wanted everything to be perfect.

John gently reminded me that his own maternal grandfather was Hispanic, which made John a quarter Hispanic himself. He actually knew something about the culture in spite of carrying an Irish last name; he grew up in it. Finally, overcoming my last fear, he pointed out that his skin was in fact browner than mine, which was not saying much as mine is the color of copy paper.

I returned to the computer and stared at the e-mail for several minutes longer. I didn't know what she was getting at behind the question she asked. People often danced around the questions they really wanted to ask, but I didn't know if this was one of those situations. I had many questions that I wanted to ask in response, but in the end decided against it. So, I simply typed "Yes" and walked away, anxiously awaiting her reply.

Chapter 23
Vuja De?

If déjà vu is the sense that something has happened before, could vuja de be the sense that something is about to happen? I waited two weeks for a reply from the county, but none came. No e-mail, no phone call, not even a flyer in the mail that announced the topic of the next monthly training class.

But on Martin Luther King Jr. Day, I was in the kitchen having breakfast when John came down. He was smiling as he slipped into the chair beside me. "I have something to tell you."

He looked like he would burst with excitement, which I found infectious. I smiled too, anxious to hear his news.

"During my Bible reading and prayer time this morning, I had a strong sense that we are going to be placed with a baby boy.

But not just any baby boy." He got up and pointed to one of the pictures I had posted on the refrigerator. "This one. I sensed that we are going to be placed with this redheaded, blue-eyed baby boy."

Now, I am usually a skeptic. But not this time. I didn't know if it was because John was so serious about what he said, or if it was because I wanted it to be true, but I believed wholeheartedly what John had told me. And for the next few days, every time I looked at that picture, I smiled, knowing that he was on his way.

Work that Friday was the only thing that had distracted my thoughts from the little boy I was sure we'd adopt. Sometime around mid-morning, I answered the phone. "Julie?" asked the caller.

"Yes."

"This is Karen from the county."

"Oh, hi Karen. How are you?"

"Well, it's kind of been a busy week here at the county...." She continued to speak.

But suddenly, it occurred to me that Karen has never called me at work. Karen has never called except to return my call. But I didn't call—I gasped. Could it be? My heart began to race. Adrenaline overtook me and I didn't trust my voice, so I spoke as slowly and deliberately as I could, "Karen, are you calling because you have a baby for us?!" I was shaking.

She laughed because I finally realized what was happening. "Yes, we have a newborn, Caucasian baby boy. Here is his situation...." She told me the story behind his placement into foster care and why the caseworkers believed he would be a candidate for adoption. I listened intently, barely hearing her above my rapid pulse. I had a couple of questions, which she answered, then finally said, "But here's the thing, Julie. He is ready to be released from the hospital and must be picked up today by two o'clock. I need to know right now if you and John want to take him. If not, I need to find him another home. So, would you talk to John and call me right back?"

"Karen, I am sure John will agree."

"Okay, but talk to him and call me back. I need to make sure you both know the situation and are consenting."

I hung up and immediately called John's cell phone. He didn't answer. I called again. Again, no answer. I attempted several more calls, one after the other. After no success, I called the office. "Trish, this is Julie. I am urgently looking for John. Do you know where he is?"

"Let me check his calendar. Hang on." The few seconds she was gone seemed like eternity. "He's on a job site and isn't expected to be back until after lunch."

My heart sank. After lunch would be too late! I had waited years for this moment, but I felt the opportunity would slip from my grasp if John couldn't be reached soon to consent to the placement. I began to cry and blubbered the situation aloud to Trish....

"Let me see what I can do, Julie." And in that moment, she held all my hope.

Chapter 24
Ready, Set, Go

For the next twenty minutes, I paced and fretted and trembled at the office. I continued to neurotically call John's cell phone and continued to get his voice mail. I was beginning to fear that we'd have to pass on this baby and our only opportunity at parenthood this far.

Finally, however, the phone rang and it was John. His meeting ended unexpectedly, and he returned to the office to a chorus of congratulations and a round of hugs and handshakes.

I didn't get to break the news to him, but I did fill in the details. "Karen called and said there was a newborn, Caucasian baby boy available. He is a preemie, born four weeks early, but still healthy. She said his birth mom is a fifteen-year-old runaway, whose dad is supposed to have custody of her. Anyway, the baby has not been exposed to drugs, that they know of, and has had limited if any alcohol exposure. The county does know the identity of the birth father. He is nineteen-years-old and works part-time at an auto body shop."

"Why does the county think this baby is eligible for adoption?" John interrupted.

"Well, that's the thing. Karen said that the birth mom and birth dad grew up together. In fact, they are step siblings. Her mom and his dad are married, and the county thinks the judge will see the situation as incest."

"But, to be clear, the birth mother and birth father aren't related by blood, right?" John clarified.

"Right. The other thing is that the birth father is nineteen years old and the birth mother is a minor. There is an issue with that as well. So, to sum it up, the county is going to the judge with two arguments. First, they grew up in the same house as siblings, which makes the situation incest. And secondly, he is considered an adult and she is a fifteen-year-old minor. That is younger than the age of consent, which the county will argue is statutory rape. They have set the court date for Thursday. Do you feel comfortable taking him?"

"Well, yeah, if the county thinks they have a strong case, then *YES!* But why will it take almost a week to go before the judge?"

"I don't know. I guess that's his first opening. So, is our answer yes?"

"YES!"

"Good! I think so too. I am so excited!" By that time, I was squealing in a pitch that only dogs could hear. "There is one more thing, though. Karen said the baby is being released from the hospital today and needs to be picked up at two o'clock. That's when a caseworker will be there to sign the discharge papers and give us his file. She also said to bring a car seat."

"Two o'clock?! That's in less than three hours, and we don't have any supplies at home to care for a newborn baby, let alone a car seat!" I imagined that my engineer-husband was grieving the loss of a Gantt chart to prepare for the arrival of our baby. I mean, he was okay with spontaneity as long as he knew to expect it.

"The county certainly wasn't kidding when they said that sometimes they called foster parents on short notice," he mused.

"Okay, look, I'm going to leave here and head to Target to get what we might need. All we need are bottles, diapers and formula, right? Oh, and clothes and bath supplies and—oh, yeah, a car seat." The room spun. "How about you just meet me there? We should be able to get all we need between the two of us, right?" It would be the blind leading the blind.

We were going from zero to family in less than three hours, and there was so much to do. I was sick to my stomach. *Were we ready for this?*

Ready, set, go!

Chapter 25
The Pickup

Before heading to the store, I made two more phone calls. The first was to my Mom, announcing her new grandbaby. The second call was to my sister, Kathy. I was hoping she would be available to meet me at Target to pick out items for the baby. She was an expert shopper, and I didn't have much time.

I'd struck gold. She was eager to help and we agreed to meet in twenty minutes. The adrenaline rush I was on had worn off on my drive to the store, and by the time I got there, I only had energy to push the cart. I'm sure we looked like a couple of women casually shopping for baby items. But from my perspective, it felt like we were on a game show (You have ten minutes to get all the supplies you need to care for a newborn child. The contestant who finishes first wins the contents of the basket. And...go!). I mean, I pushed the cart, but Kathy was recklessly heaving stuff off the shelves by the armful, leaving behind destruction that rivaled Armageddon. Well, that's how it seemed to me and my checkbook, anyway, in my post-adrenaline fog.

In the parking lot, I realized I didn't have a car seat. But Kathy had already thought about that and we headed over to Babies "R" Us. Kathy already knew which car seat we should have, one that snapped into a car base and stroller, and she gifted it to us for the occasion. Running short on time, I hugged her and thanked her and we agreed that the family would meet at her house later to meet our little guy. Then, John and I headed to the hospital.

Though it was January, the sun was strong and the day was warm, melting off the dirty snow. We arrived at the hospital holding hands, and John swung the empty car seat in his other. We met the caseworker at the nurse's station on the third floor. She had already begun the paperwork, but still had documents for us to sign. She excused herself, as she had another appointment, and left us in the care of the nurse.

"Well, are you ready to meet your baby?" she asked. I took a deep breath and blew out my anxiety. *Can I do this? Will he like me? Will I be a good mom?* I couldn't remember being so nervous.

She pushed open the door and at the end of the room under the window was a little fellow already in a car seat, sleeping. We made our way over to him. He was so beautiful and tiny and peaceful. I couldn't wait to get my hands on him!

Fortunately, the nurse urged us to wake him because he needed to eat before we left.

I told John to go first. He lifted the baby out of the car seat and cradled him in his arms. The baby's eyes opened briefly and he crinkled his forehead at the disturbance, but quickly settled back to sleep. I would have been happy to let him sleep, as he and John seemed so relaxed with one another, but the nurse said it was feeding time, so wake him up!

We murmured softly to him and timidly shook his shoulder, but the nurse was having none of that. She took the baby from John and ordered me to wash my hands. Then, she put the baby in his hospital crib-cart and instructed me to undress him to his onesie, explaining that he wouldn't sleep if he wasn't warm. *Made sense to me.* I washed up and approached the crib-cart. It was finally my turn to hold the baby, so I blew on my cold hands, rubbed them together and reached for him.
However, the nurse stopped me abruptly. I was spreading bacteria by blowing on my hands, she said, and therefore needed to wash again. She sent me back to the sink, and I thought I heard John giggle.

I scrubbed like a surgeon and again approached the baby, careful not to touch anything that would infect him. I pulled off his knit cap first and underneath was a shock of soft, red hair. Next, I unwrapped his receiving blanket and unsnapped his pajamas. He was born prematurely, and as I gently pulled out each limb, I noticed how skinny he really was, barely over five pounds. His newborn complexion was ruddy, but he also suffered from jaundice, so his wrinkly skin was slightly orange in color. Then, I peeked down his back and saw his entire body was covered with blond hair, which according to the nurse was a sign of his preterm birth. In all, he looked like a cross between a peach and a Shar-Pei puppy, but I thought he was just beautiful as he kicked and squirmed and peeped at me from beneath his furrowed brow.

When he was stripped down to his onesie and socks, the nurse declared he was ready to eat and handed me a bottle, which she showed John how to mix. The feeding went smoothly, and having eaten and burped, he slipped off to sleep once again. So, we dressed him and belted him into our car seat. We then thanked the nurse for her instruction and time and left with our new little baby.

In the car, John and I took a moment to offer God a prayer of thanks for filling our hearts and fulfilling our dream. It was already better than we ever expected it could be. Then, we headed off, the three of us, a family.

Chapter 26
A Warm Reception

As planned, we took our new baby to Kathy's house, where my sisters prepared a celebratory dinner and my Mom singlehandedly blessed us with more gifts than we would receive from a baby shower. Literally, we left with half a dozen onesies, sleepers, outfits, and diapers in every size up to one year. As only a mom would know the pain of her daughter's infertility, my mom also knew the significance of this baby to me. The gifts were her way of showing her excitement for me and also her acceptance of a baby not born to me. In her way, she was telling me that this baby is her grandchild—not her adopted grandchild—and she would be as proud and fiercely protective of him as her other grandchildren, if not more so.

My mom was the first to take the baby, barely letting us through the door before she snatched him from his car seat.

All four nieces crowded around her on the club chair to peek at the new baby. She secured him on her lap and began to undress him, much like I did at the hospital. Then she examined him from head to toe making comments about everything from his hair ("Red, like John's.") to his skin ("Jaundice, but that will go away.") to his length ("I think you guys have a tall son here, God bless him."). She did everything she could to wake him, and when he furrowed his brow and opened his eyes at the disturbance, she hooted with delight. Then, she passed him off to be held by each member of the family, my sisters, their husbands, and all four nieces while John and I ate.

Mom sat back in her chair, sipped her coffee and asked, "What are you going to name him?"

I glanced at John. We wanted to name him Christopher after my dad, who would have burst with pride over the gesture. I imagined he would have bored the neighbors with his story about his first grandson being named after him. But I was hesitant to say it, because although my Dad passed away over two years ago, he was still greatly missed. We never got together without feeling his absence, and speaking his name would make the evening bittersweet, even though I intended to honor him. Furthermore, I believed that Kathy wanted to name her son after Dad, but after two daughters, I wasn't sure if she and Mike were planning on more children, so my announcement might be stepping on her toes.

"Well, we thought we'd name him Christopher," I said

cautiously. The muttering around the room stopped for a moment, and I could feel the weight of bereavement descend on us. I imagined that everyone, even Julia, who was two-and-a-half when he died, was recollecting some memory of him. We adored him, that godly man who had endless patience for his wife, three daughters, and four granddaughters. He would have been thrilled to welcome a grandson, just as he was thrilled to welcome sons-in-law.

"If that's okay with you," I added, looking at Kathy. She was wiping tears from her eyes when she looked up and smiled and nodded at me.

"He would love that," she said. And in that moment, I was grateful to be blessed with a close-knit, generous family who truly loved and supported one another. And I knew that that was how I wanted to raise my son.

Chapter 27
You Are My Sunshine

Even though we waited months to be placed with a baby, we hadn't put up a crib. I wasn't sure if it was because we didn't actually believe we would be placed with a baby or because it was too painful for an infertile couple to look at an empty crib. Nevertheless, it was late on Friday night and we'd had such an emotional day that neither John nor I wanted to go home and assemble one. We were discussing that when Kathy said she might be able to help. She disappeared into the basement and returned with a cradle and mattress. The legs needed assembling, but the cradle was in one piece and would be fine for the night.

We said our good-byes to the family, loaded the cradle and the baby and left. Ever the planner, John forecasted the rest of the night: We would get home and set the cradle on the floor in our bedroom, put the baby to bed and be ready to feed him again in three hours. *Three hours, ugh.* That sounded so painful after the roller-coaster day we'd had. But we both wanted to give him his first bottle at home, so we agreed to get up together when the alarm went off.

When the alarm rang out, Christopher was barely grunting. I felt like I had just laid down, and my body positively ached from exhaustion. Any other day, I would have sobbed at the thought of getting up in this shape, but tonight sheer excitement launched me off the bed.

John carefully carried the baby downstairs and I held him while John made the bottle. He was so sleepy. The nurse said he might want to sleep longer than the three to four hours between feedings, but as a preemie and a newborn, he needed the nourishment. So to wake him up, I undressed him, once again, down to his onesie. He looked so innocent and perfect and beautiful, this little gift for which I prayed so hard. I couldn't get enough of him. I closed my eyes and nuzzled his limp little neck, drinking in the sweet, pure smell of new life. *Mmm, was there anything more fragrant?* Then, I dotted his head and fingers and toes with soft kisses, rubbed his back and sang:

You are my sunshine, my only sunshine. You make me happy when skies are grey. You'll never know, dear, how much I love you. Please don't take my sunshine away.

I already loved this little being with all my heart. I'd guessed when you wanted something so badly for so long, it was easy to latch on to the dream. I felt like I was living the emotional equivalent of a long-waiting patient who had finally received his organ transplant. Life was about to begin, and it was good. John returned with the bottle and I relinquished the baby. He ate with little interest and had to be chided several times to keep feeding. He didn't seem to mind being cold and half naked in the middle of January. He only wanted to sleep. Having finished eating and burping, John changed his diaper. Then the two of them reclined on the chair, Christopher on John's chest, and both fell asleep.

I draped a fleece blanket over the two of them, then collapsed on the sofa myself, pulling another over me. The emotions of the day left me drained, barely able to move. But my heart was full, overflowing with happiness and the blessing of this little life. We finally got the family we had always wanted, and I finally became a mom, the best title in the world. I smiled to myself and a tear slipped from my eye and disappeared into the pillow. I gave God a silent prayer of thanks. How could I possibly deserve this?

Chapter 28
The Visit

And so the week continued. John took the week off work, and together we gave Christopher every feeding, every diaper change, and every bath. To the outsider, our behavior must have bordered on fanatical. We threw blankets over the windows and slept when the baby slept, so it was no surprise that we were sleeping when the doorbell rang at 4 p.m. on Tuesday. John's coworkers had stopped by to bring us dinner and gifts. It must have seemed rude to them that John greeted them at the door without inviting them in, but the only beings nesting inside had sleepy sand in the corners of their eyes and zoo breath radiating from their lips. Less than ideal company, really.

We finally emerged from our cocoon on Wednesday, as we were required to take the baby to his scheduled visitation with his birth mother. We were told to check in at the waiting room and a caseworker would come and take the baby to meet with his birth mother. Easy enough.

To tell the truth, the waiting room looked eerily similar to the DMV. They must have used the same interior decorator. Chairs lined the walls of the long, tiled room and the only decoration was an analog clock that hung high on the long wall. To the right of the clock was a security-coded door that I assumed led to the visitation rooms. Here at the entry, a secretary sat in a booth behind what I imagined was bulletproof glass. A speaker was drilled through the glass and I gave our names and "visitation" as the reason for our visit.

We took our seats and set the baby's car seat on the floor. I surveyed the room. There were several women of various ages who sat with children beside them or on their laps, but nobody was chatting with her neighbor. I was about to mention that to John when a squeal of delight pierced the silence. A young, excited redheaded girl charged toward us with her eyes on the baby's car seat. Two men followed behind her.

She introduced herself as the baby's birth mother, dropped to the floor and began to free him from the car seat. I shot John a look. *What was the protocol? Should we ask for ID?* As an afterthought, she introduced the tall man as her dad and the blond man as her boyfriend, the baby's father. Then, she rose from the floor with the baby, indicated she brought a bottle to feed him, and made her way to the far corner of the room to begin their visit.

John and I looked at each other. *What just happened there?* I hoped she was in fact the birth mother. I mean, that could be really awkward! We decided that since we were legally responsible for the little guy, we should stick around until the caseworker arrived.

Birth mom retrieved a bottle from her bag, and she and birth dad sat head-to-head over the baby while he ate. Mom commented over and over about how big he had gotten in a week and grandpa predicted the baby would be an athlete, tall and muscular.

The caseworker finally arrived and relieved us of our supervision duties. At that, John and I left to find a coffee shop. We sized up the visit, and I confessed to John that I had mixed thoughts about this baby. This girl didn't look like a flaky runaway to me, although I didn't know if I could identify a runaway if I saw one. But furthermore, her relationship with her boyfriend seemed genuine and sweet, not what I would have considered statutory rape. And her dad seemed to be kind and patient and supportive of them both. Hey, grandpa took off work to come to a visit he wasn't required to attend. That showed solidarity. For a moment, I glimpsed a loving, close-knit future for this young family.

Suddenly, I had an uneasy feeling about the permanency of our placement, and John agreed. He said if he were the judge presiding over this case, he would consider giving this family a chance to raise this little guy. Their showing up at this visit and their behavior proved they would do anything to keep their family together.

With mixed feelings, we made our way back to the county. The birth parents were already prepared to return the baby, and birth dad approached John with an outstretched hand. He shook John's hand and graciously thanked us for taking such great care of his son, while birth mom buckled the baby back into the car seat. They locked hands, thanked us again and promised to see us at the next visit. Then, they left.

I watched them walk to their car and drive away. It seemed to take them an eternity. And for the first time, I wondered if this was really our forever baby.

Chapter 29
The Cruelest Call

Unsettled feelings still gripped me the morning after the baby's visit with his birth parents, but I was certain to get an update on the case that day, as all parties were due in court. According to Karen, the county took custody of the baby for two reasons. They believed incest was involved between the birth parents and they believed bio dad committed statutory rape. For the baby's well-being, he needed to be removed from the situation. Now, it was incumbent upon the county to defend those charges to the court with the birth parents present.

Our caseworker told us she would call when she had news, and when the phone rang, my heart thumped.

"Julie, this is Beth from the county. I just left court."

"Yes," I replied, "thank you for calling so quickly."

"Well, the birth parents both appeared before the judge. And just to recap the history, bio mom's mother and bio dad's father are married. So, the baby's birth parents grew up together as stepsiblings. Currently, bio mom's father has legal custody of her, but she keeps running away from him and going back to her mother's house, so she can be with her stepbrother, the baby's father."

"Right. At least that's what we were told."

"Well, the baby's biological father is nineteen years old and the biological mother is fifteen. Because of that, the judge ordered bio dad to be taken into custody and charged with statutory rape. He will be indicted in criminal court, likely post bail and return to live at his father's house until trial. At that point, if he is found guilty, he will have to register as a sex offender. That was one of the reasons for taking the baby into custody.

"The other reason was the suspected incest. The judge didn't agree that incest was involved as there was no blood relation between the two birth parents. So, as for bio mom, the judge decided that she was simply the victim of the alleged sex offender." She paused for a moment and then took a deep breath. "Julie, the judge ordered that she be allowed to parent her baby. It means that the baby will be returned to his birth mother."

I felt like I had just been slapped. I looked over at John, who was feeding the baby on the sofa in the next room. He raised his eyebrows as if to say, "Well, what's the good news?" I managed a half-smile, but struggled to keep my tears from surfacing.

"But she's a runaway, Beth. How can she parent this child?" I managed.

"I know. And, since she is a known runaway—running to the house where her alleged sex-offender-boyfriend will be living—she will be placed in a mutual home with the baby. That is a foster home that will accept a teen mom and her baby. They'll live there together. Which means the county is taking custody of bio mom as well as baby. That way, they can keep her safe from her alleged sex-offender-boyfriend too." She paused.

"Beth, I don't understand. I thought this was supposed to be an airtight case. When Karen called us with the placement, she was certain this baby would become available for adoption."

"Well, all I can say is sometimes the judge doesn't agree with our assessment. And in the end, it is his ruling that matters." I summed it up. "So that's it? We are going to lose this baby."

"Yes," she said. Then quickly added, "But if she can't parent him or she runs away again and he comes back into the system, you guys will get him back." She was trying to soften the blow or maybe give us a spark of hope. Maybe she was trained to say something like this so foster parents like me didn't go psycho and harm someone. Whatever the case, I was angry and devastated and powerless.

And light-headed. I thought I might need to put my head between my knees. *How could this be happening?* This was all too surreal. I leaned on the counter to support my quivering legs.

"One more thing, Julie." *There's more?!* "It is going to take a little while for us to find a mutual home for bio mom and her baby." Oh, he was *her* baby now. When we were first called, he was *our* baby. The caseworker and the nurse congratulated us on *our* baby at the hospital. How subtle the change. I was spiraling into despair. She continued, "We need you to bring him back to the county on Wednesday at two o'clock. We'll do the transfer then."

"Another week?" This was beyond belief!

"Yes, we need to locate a foster home that will take them both. There just aren't that many that are certified for mother and child. And stability is in the baby's best interest. We don't want to move him now just to move him again in a week. Do you see what I mean?" Of course, I did. The one thing that was taught over and over in the classes was the need for stability and its impact on attachment.

It was the final blow.

I barely managed to grunt "uh-huh" before I closed my eyes and let the tears stream down my cheeks. In one phone call, I went from being "Mom" to being childless again. And what was worse was this baby that I already loved was going to continue to live in our house and in my arms for the next week, his looming departure being a cruel reminder of my deficiency.

We were defenseless. We had no claim to this baby biologically or legally. And if we ever chose to be placed again—which I couldn't imagine—I felt we needed to comply with their terms. We would keep the baby and care for him another week, even as our hearts were breaking.

I agreed to everything she asked and hung up the phone.

I turned and looked at John. He was snuggling the baby on his chest and they were settling in for a nap.

It was left to me to crush his hopes….

Chapter 30
Comfort in the Storm

For the first time since we were placed with the baby, I didn't get up with John to feed him.

"I want you to get a good night's sleep, especially after the day we've had," he told me. I didn't argue with him. After being told that we'd have to give up the baby, I cried most of the day. Fortunately, John had been there when I took the call. He understood the process and the risks of foster parenting.

My mom, on the other hand, indignantly remarked that the county couldn't wave the promise of parenthood in front of people and then treat them like glorified babysitters. "It's rubbing salt in the wound," she went on, "because babysitters make more money! Baiting and switching, that's what they're doing. It's just a cheap way for them to get couples to care for these babies until they return them to their parents."

I didn't have the energy to defend the county and I certainly didn't have the energy to listen to my mom's rants. I promised to call her later, and hung up.

As I sat on the sofa, I felt truly defeated. Since John and I were married, we watched my Dad lose his long battle with cancer, we spent months having our fertility tested and many more months enduring fruitless fertility treatments, and now our hope of adopting through foster care had been snuffed out as well. I had hit rock bottom. And I was tired.

John would feed the baby at two a.m. and again at six a.m. and then wake me before he went to work. He had taken a week's vacation to be home with me and our "forever" baby, and I could see no point in his staying home any longer when we were going to have to give him back. But the truth was that I was dreading being home by myself with this baby that we weren't keeping. I really didn't want to get any more attached to him than I already was, as selfish as that sounded. This little man came into our house and promised to make us a family. And we were a family for a short time and it was fantastic! He changed our whole dynamic. The thought of going back to being childless brought me to my knees.

John woke me the next morning after he fed the baby. It was after eight and I was suddenly alarmed. "What's going on?" I asked, "Why are you still home? Is the baby okay?"

"Everything is fine. I just decided that I would stay with you until Wednesday, when we take him back."

I rubbed the sleepy sand from my eyes. "John, you have already blown through a week of vacation time. You only have one left and it is January. I can take care of him myself."

"I know you can take care of him yourself, but I don't want you to have to. I am going to help you feed him and bathe him and change him till Wednesday. I don't want you to have to go through this by yourself." He smiled as best he could through misty eyes and brushed my hair off my face. "I don't want you to hurt all by yourself. I want to be here for you and with you right now.... I love you. I am not going to leave you."

I thought about those words. God himself said "I will never leave you nor forsake you." And I felt strangely comforted. At that moment, I could see no hope in our adopting, no hope in our becoming parents at all. This baby was leaving us and it was unlikely we'd choose to do this again. But here was John, my best friend, and he was sticking with me.

"Now get up. I got you breakfast from Cracker Barrel, your favorite...."

Chapter 31
Broken

We said good-bye to my Dad on a strikingly beautiful day. It was early June and gardens everywhere were beautifully lush and green. The cemetery smelled of freshly mowed lawn and the bushes and trees were awash with new blooms offering up a visual treat. As we stood around his grave, mature trees swayed in the breeze and cast shadows over the crowd like a canopy of lace. Somewhere nearby birds practiced their melodies, dogs yipped wildly, and impish children snickered and squealed. And above it all, the sun flooded the earth with its light and life. And I resented all of it. *How dare creation rejoice when we were bidding my dad farewell!*

We would say good-bye to baby Christopher on an equally breathtaking but far different day. The talons of winter had gripped the state for many days, engulfing it in temperatures so cold and dry that moisture from my lips vaporized into soft puffs. Grey clouds and thin fog struggled to restrain the sun, but in the end, glorious rays of soft light caressed the lazy snowflakes, causing them to twinkle and shimmer and flitter weightlessly, like glitter through the dry air. Indeed, Mother Nature had lured her offspring into a deep and silent slumber. A still serenity cloaked the atmosphere, and in all, proved as enchanting as any fantasy or fable or fairy tale.

But this good-bye would not be marked with the cheeky evidence of life and merriment that surrounded my dad's. This good-bye would only be attended by John and me, two people who only wished to become parents. And failed. Yet again.

I sipped my tea at the window and thought about the reaction of our friends at church when we told them we had to give up this baby. Many kind people expressed their sadness and showered us with prayers and hugs, but one gentleman simply stated that we knew this could happen when we became foster parents. Why were we so sad?

Indeed, we did know that this could happen, in our heads but not our hearts. I thought about what we had to do that afternoon. We were court ordered to give back the baby. *What mother on earth does that?* And then it was confirmed to me: I was not this baby's mother. I loved him from the moment I held him. I fed him and nurtured him and dreamed for him. But I had no claim to him.

And once again, I was reminded of my failings. I was infertile, plain and simple. Billions of women throughout history had given birth, a task set aside by God specifically for women. But not me. Was it because of my sins? Have I not asked forgiveness for something? Sadly, I fully understood what it was to be barren, the curse and the shame of it. Infertility was not simply a biblical phenomenon. To be judged unworthy of children was every bit as humiliating and dishonorable now as it was then.

I did everything in my power to become a mother: acupuncture, nutrition, drugs, fertility treatments, and now a failed adoption. It still wasn't enough. Now, I was out of options and out of ideas and out of energy. I dropped to the floor and allowed myself a good, cleansing bawl.

I didn't know how long I sat there and cried, but something told me it was time to get up. We had to relinquish this baby today, and I had no idea how I was going to find the strength to do that.

Finally, the only thing I could think to do was to pray. "Salve to the soul," my dad would say. So, I choked out the only words that would come, "Lord, please be with us.... We need you now…"

Chapter 32
Despair in the Air

It was time to get the baby ready. I asked John to pack the diaper bag while I gave the little guy a bath. Christopher loved bath time more than anything. He loved tummy time the least. In fact, the moment he was placed on his tummy, he would start screaming like a banshee, all red-faced and flailing limbs. But bath time was his favorite. So, I put his plastic tub into the sink and ran a bubble bath. I gently scrubbed his feet and legs and knees, kissing each as I went. Inevitably, I ended up with bubbles on my nose. Working all the way up to his head, I sang:

Head, shoulders, knees and toes. Head, shoulders, knees and toes. Eyes and ears and a mouth and nose. Head, shoulders, knees and toes.

Once I had gotten to his head, I lathered up his red hair, then ran a gentle stream of warm water from the faucet and rinsed. He responded by rolling his head back and forth, sometimes tipping it backward. He couldn't get enough. It reminded me of a puppy nuzzling up to get his head scratch. He loved the feel of the running water on his head; it relaxed him. I thought about how this would be the last bath I would give him and began to tear up. I just loved this mini-man. *I can't let my mind go there now. I have to finish getting ready!* But the tears remained there, just beneath the surface, waiting for me to let my guard down.

I lifted him from the tub onto a towel and wrapped him so completely that only his bright eyes were visible under the layers of terry cloth. Having already set out his after-bath necessities, I carried him to the bed, toweled him down and began to slather him with lotion, which always reminded me of turtle wax for some reason. *His last waxing.* I couldn't help but go there again. *Every little task with my little ninja-turtle-man would be the last. The last feeding, the last diaper change, the last bath, the last kiss, the last snuggle, the last touch. And then…the last memory.* I didn't even bother trying to stop them this time. I laid down beside the baby, played with his fingers and let the waiting tears flow. This was it. There would be no celebrating his first solid foods, his first crawl, his first tooth, or his first birthday. No celebrating whatsoever. The tears poured out, but they didn't cleanse. They didn't cleanse the underlying issues of infertility and hopelessness. How could they? That's all we'd be left with when we relinquished this baby.

Just then, John came into the room with misty, red eyes. He had a sheet of paper in his hands.

"Tell me how this sounds," he said.

"Dear parents, we are the foster parents of your beautiful baby boy. He is a wonderful baby and I am sure you are proud of him. But we understand from the caseworkers that you, Dad, are unfortunately facing criminal charges and that you, Mom, will be removed from your home and placed in foster care with the baby. This is not an ideal situation any way you look at it. We are prepared to offer you $10,000 to give up your parental rights and allow us to adopt your baby. That way, Mom, you won't have to go to foster care. And, Dad, you can weather the storm of your trial, and at the end you two can be together and have more children down the line. Meanwhile, you know that good people are raising your son. Here is my number XXX-XXX-XXXX. Let's talk. Sincerely, John and Julie Burke.

"What do you think? I thought I would tuck it deep into the pocket of the diaper bag."

What did I think!? My tears stopped mid-flow. I snatched the letter from his hands and read it myself. I was dumbstruck. I understood grief, which could make you do some crazy things, but you just didn't compound it with stupidity. I could feel the heat rising from my feet as I looked at John for a long moment. Incredible. He was serious!

"Have you hit your head?" I barked. Nothing trumps sorrow like anger.

"No. What's the problem?"

"Well, let me see," I mockingly rubbed at an imaginary beard. "I am pretty sure it is illegal to offer a bribe and I'm quite sure it is illegal to buy babies, John! Have you heard of black market adoption? If you put that letter in the diaper bag, you might find yourself sharing a jail cell with bio dad for a few weeks before you are hauled off to Sing Sing. And if you put my name on it, I'll be charged as an accessory to the crime, sentenced to probation, and forced to do community service, if I'm lucky. But if I'm unlucky, I could end up doing hard labor on a chain gang in the humidity in the middle of West Texas. On the bright side, though, I could learn a new life skill, like making license plates! I hear it's in high demand. In any event, when I finish my sentence and reapply to adopt, I think agencies will have a hard time getting past the word "felon" on my application. But, I could be wrong." I rolled my eyes. I couldn't believe I was having this conversation.

"Nobody will know. I'll just hand the diaper bag directly to the birth parents and they can read the letter when they get home."

"*Nobody will know?*" I wasn't usually the voice of reason, so this was all new territory for me. "John, do you think you are the first foster parent to dream this up? I am sure the county has caught people in a bribe more than once. I can assure you that they will not be handling the disruption like they did visitation for this very reason. It would be too tempting for foster parents to prey on birth parents' weaknesses. Foster parents get a baby and bio parents get money for their next hit? That's quite an exchange. No, the caseworkers will be digging through every inch of the diaper bag. And they'll search the baby too. Trust me. Surely, we haven't sunk that far." I ripped the letter into the tiniest pieces possible.

He hugged me and held me a long time. I knew he was grieving too. He was grieving the loss of this baby, the loss of our little family, and the loss of my dream, which he felt responsible to deliver but helpless to do so. He was struggling against despair and defeat just as I was. I needed to extend him some grace. My mom would say you shouldn't be held responsible for the things you said or did during a period of grief. It was like being judged on your worst day.

And believe me, if this wasn't our worst day, it was certainly a close second.

Chapter 33
Call Me Mara

"Call me Mara, for the Almighty has made my life very bitter."
—The Book of Ruth

We parked in the lot under a blanket of grey clouds. John slipped his hand over mine and prayed that we would have strength for the coming relinquishment. Together, we decided that we would make this good-bye brief, as brief as we possibly could anyway. If there was one thing we learned by working with the county, it was that we didn't have control over anything.

John got out of the car and removed the baby's car seat and bag from the back. He was sleeping, this easygoing cherub that I would miss so much. I wondered how the disruption might affect him. Ours was the only home he had known, after all.

He may not have been born to me, but we had already created a bond and a rhythm. For example, I always rubbed his chin before I fed him because it woke him up and caused him to lick his lips. I took that to mean he was getting himself ready to feed. Who would know to do that now? Who would know that he liked his back rubbed, not patted, when he was being burped? And that he liked the warm water to run directly on his head during his bath? Maybe it didn't matter. I was sure he would develop new rhythms, but would he be anxious in the meantime? It all weighed on my mind. I worried for this little guy, for his well-being and his future.

John held the baby in his car seat and I held his bag. With our free hands, we took hold of one another, as if the magnitude of our upcoming duty might overwhelm us individually. We signed in, went to the visitation room, and requested our caseworker.

Two caseworkers arrived within minutes and led us to the only table in the visitation room, where we all stood. While John took the baby from his car seat, I briefly reviewed the baby's paperwork with the caseworkers.

"He had been seen by a pediatrician on this date," I pointed to my notes on the paper the caseworker retrieved from the notebook. "The pediatrician's name, address, and phone number are there, and he recommends the baby be seen again in three weeks. Oh, that page is his medicine history. It is blank because he is not on any prescriptions and we didn't need to give him Tylenol or ibuprofen." Papers were being haphazardly shuffled back and forth and I did my best to identify each as she skimmed over them. "Those are his birth records from the hospital. They should be given to his new pediatrician. That is his health care card. And finally, that is his feeding schedule with some tips on what works if he stops sucking or falls asleep during his bottle. Also, we brought all the cans of formula that we had. They are in the bag." And with that, the other caseworker opened each pocket and emptied the entire contents of the bag onto the table. They recorded an inventory of the items on another sheet of paper.

Having already said his good-bye, my emotional husband handed me the baby. I lifted him up so we were face-to-face, almost nose-to-nose. He was squirming as a result of the disturbance, but I wanted him to hear me. I looked straight at him, as if my stare would pierce his understanding.

"I love you so much, sweet boy. Please know, you will always be in my heart." I kissed his forehead and gave him one last nuzzle, tears streaming down my cheeks and onto the back of his sleeper. I wanted to hold him there forever, squeezing him until I knew my love made an imprint on his heart, made a difference in his life. But the truth was he would never even know, let alone remember, how much I loved him. And that was the most bitter aspect of all. Then I kissed his ear and through a broken whisper managed, "May God bless you and keep you close, mini-man." I was on the verge of a breakdown.

And with that, I looked at the caseworker. She took the cue and stepped up to take him from my arms, then from the room, and ultimately, from our lives. We weren't even entitled to updates about him now that he was out of our custody.

And just like that, he was gone.

Anxious to distance ourselves from the ordeal, John and I joined hands and lumbered to the car with an empty car seat, the only remnant of our journey. We sat there for a minute, drying our eyes and blowing our noses, bewildered by the highs and lows of the last couple of weeks.

"Home?" John asked as he started the car.

"No!" I couldn't bear the thought of returning to our home without our son. It was where my dream came alive for a few short weeks, where my love had known a new dimension. How do you go back to black-and-white when you have seen color? Or return to a single instrument when you have experienced a symphony? I knew his memory would haunt me at home, and I wasn't ready to face that. I was hurting and empty and in need of comfort. I decided to go to the only place where I could be unguardedly glum and weepy and still be accepted and loved. "I want to see my mom."

Chapter 34
My Cup Runneth Over

Mom met me at the door with an all-encompassing hug, one that took me back to my childhood and made me a little girl again. No judgment, no "where to go from here," or "you should have done this instead," just medicinal mother-love washing over the suffering and restoring well-being. A lifetime of support and loyalty and truth undergirded that embrace and allowed me to be raw and exposed with her in a way I couldn't be with anyone else. And she cried with me, cleansing, therapeutic tears from the one woman who bolstered and nurtured my dreams like they were her own. I truly believed she mourned as deeply as I did.

She led me into the family room of Kathy's house where the whole family had gathered. Mary was at the kitchen table with my four nieces, who were coloring the sympathy cards they had made for us out of construction paper. I knew it was her idea to have the girls make cards. It was her way of comforting me, through them. If she had hugged me directly, she wouldn't be able to recover her composure. Best to move on toward healing. One by one, Mary prodded each girl into presenting her card to John and me with a hug and some version of "I'm sorry you lost your baby, Aunt Julie and Uncle John, and my only boy cousin. I love you." The girls' ages ranged between four and nine years old and the pictures on their cards ranged from rainbows and sunshine to babies with blue diapers, crying their eyes out. Oh, how I loved these girls! I made a mental note to host a Saturday sleepover at Aunt Julie's and Uncle John's house really soon, where the girls loved to have a fashion show (in their pajamas), a photo shoot, and a "spontaneous" dance party, which culminated with a Disney princess movie and popcorn and sleeping bodies all over the floor of my living room. We would, then, get up on Sunday morning, play a session of hair salon and head out to Sunday school, followed by lunch and home to the parents. Every sleepover was exactly the same because the girls liked the routine, even at an irregular event, like our sleepovers.

I had gotten up to get some dinner, which Kathy and Mary cooked and arranged all over the countertops. Kathy slid into the chair beside me at the table and handed me a greeting card. I opened it and read it, noting it was from Kathy, Mike, and the girls. But, inside the card was a poem on laminated card stock the size of a credit card. It read:

When the world lies heavy on your heart…

Remember that I'm here and I care…
I won't pretend to understand what you're going through, but I'll
share it…

I won't attempt to comfort you with empty words or promises, but
I'll pray for you and hold you in my heart…

If there's anything I can do or if you simply need someone to lean
on, I hope you'll come to me—I want to help…
B.J. Hoff

It made me cry, of course, but Kathy interrupted my moment.

"Did you recognize it?" she asked.

"What, the poem? No, should I have?"

"You sent me that card ten years ago when I was at my lowest point."

"You kept it all this time?"

"Yes. I kept it in my wallet and now I want you to have it," she replied.

My heart was touched and I didn't know what to say. Some poets and experts believe that love is shown in grand gestures, such as large bouquets of roses and precious jewels, but that's not my style. Love to me is spoken in a thousand different simple acts, such as homemade sympathy cards, genuine hugs, and memories returned at the perfect moment.

And in that split second, I realized how grateful and fortunate I was for this family with whom I was blessed. Because, with or without a child of my own, my cup overflowed.

Chapter 35
The Power of Labels

All alone, I sat there with my thoughts. As children, do we learn to live up to the labels our parents place on us, or do our parents place labels on us based on certain overarching traits?

Sometimes, Dad would proudly reminisce, "When she was a little girl, I used to wrap her thick, auburn hair around my fingers to make perfect ringlets. That's all it took. That's how I'd get her ready for Sunday school." Other times, I would hear him and Mom recall her birth and how perfectly pink her skin was. "Truly, I have never seen a more beautiful newborn baby in all my life," my Mom would say. "She looked like she was about three months old on the day she was born, not a wrinkle or a blemish." It was all true, of course, and even I, as a little girl, could see for myself Kathy's beauty, her enviable bone structure and perfectly straight teeth. She could play in the sun all day and no freckles would appear, just gloriously bronzed skin that complemented her striking green eyes. I had none of that, of course. I had simple grey eyes with strange brown dots in them, pasty-white skin, near-black hair, big bucky teeth, and skin that freckled up when I walked from the house to the mailbox. At our house, it was never expressed outright but always understood that Kathy was the "pretty one."

Now, Mary had a breeziness about her. I knew she had her intense moments, but for the most part, she was carefree, fun, and social. Academics were far down her to-do list. To her, school was just a place to socialize, right? Her laugh was so infectious that once she started, you would laugh too, even if it wasn't necessarily funny. Your laughter would make her laugh even harder, to the point that her whole body shook but no noise was actually escaping. Sometimes, she'd cry from laughing so hard. Sometimes, she'd pee herself. It was easy to see that her joy beamed from her soul. How could you not be attracted to that? Somehow, though, all that laughter seemed far from serious to my dad, who was very serious. I remembered one night when Mary was going to yet another high school basketball game. He closed his eyes and shook his head as he rubbed his fingers back and forth across his forehead, "She's boy crazy." That was all that needed to be said.

For me, the inverse was true. I was serious and book smart and made good grades. It made Dad proud; I was like him, in a way. He had graduated high school at sixteen years old, went into the Air Force from there, and then, on to college. His profession became engineering, but his passion was chess. He loved the drama, the strategizing, and the intellect of the game. My dad, the master chess player, even once played Bobby Fischer to a draw. He often took me to his Tuesday night chess club, where he would have me play some other member's son. My trouncing of the opponent would make Dad beam with pride and he would tell his buddies, "You don't have to be male to have a great mind."

Though my mind was strong, my body was weak. I was diagnosed with two chronic illnesses in my early teens. Of course, I thought my life was over. I wondered aloud to him one day about how things were going to change for me, how my life would be handicapped. He simply stated, "Your sickness won't hold you back. It may take you longer to get to where you want to go, but you can do whatever you put your mind to."

Later, when I was in college, he would stay up with me until two a.m. and quiz me for my biology exams. After cramming for six hours, I would be exhausted and whiny and complain about how I just couldn't do it. He would reply, "Yes you can. You can do whatever you put your mind to." When I couldn't decide on a major, he would say, "You can do whatever you put your mind to." When I wondered if I could land that internship in Washington, D.C., or that job in radio, he simply said, "You can do whatever you put your mind to. Work like it depends on you, and pray like it depends on God. Because it does."

He told me again and again I could accomplish anything. And then I believed it. And with his voice in my head, I accomplished all of it. I graduated from college in four years despite several hospitalizations. I was awarded the internship out of a hundred or so applicants because I did my research. Then I flew out to DC and stayed with a friend for a long weekend. I dressed up as I would for a job interview and casually dropped by the senate office to meet the intern director in a just-visiting-a-friend-and-thought-I'd-drop-by-to-meet-you (oh, by the way, I have applied for your spring internship) kind of way. Of course, once I was awarded the internship, I worked my fingers to the bone, even through the boring bits, and became the press secretary's "all-time favorite" intern. At the end of my internship, I was offered a permanent position, but I came back to Colorado instead. And I landed the job on the radio. For days, I read about techniques of successful radio broadcasters and then spent hours practicing before the open "cattle call." Research, work, and preparation (my "smarts") always worked in my favor, and I had relied on those tools to accomplish my goals.

But my goal now was to become a mom. And everything I had tried failed.

Somehow, I stumbled into that dark and lonely abyss, that cesspool, where my reality fell short of my expectation. No doing or planning or working was enough this time, and I didn't even have the energy to try again. The truth was that any possible flicker of hope would have to come looking for me. I was lost.

I couldn't say how long I sat there rehashing my failures when it finally hit me: "Pray like it depends on God. Because it does."

Chapter 36
Grasping at Hope

"Remember how he would fall asleep during his bottle and we'd have to make him a little cool to get him to eat?" I reminisced to John.

"I loved that he would cuddle up on me when he was done eating. We'd fall asleep and have a mini-nap together."

Despite our best efforts, our evening conversations eventually rolled around to recollecting memories of our weeks with Christopher. I remembered that Mom and my sisters and I did that after Dad died. We talked about how he took such great care of his chess sets, fell asleep when he sat down to watch television, and became annoyed when his hair started to gray. Somehow, talking about Dad kept him alive. It was as if we were afraid we'd forget something about him.

Likewise, John and I talked about Christopher's little habits and quirks to keep his memory fresh and to work through our grief. However, Christopher had not died. He was returned to his birth mother. And even though it felt like a death to us, our grief was shortchanged because there was no death or funeral or closure. Just loss. And it was unbearable.

"I can't do it again," I explained to John, for the millionth time since the baby left. He knew exactly what I was talking about. I couldn't go through another disrupted placement.

"I know. I can't do it either."

"We poured our hearts into that baby. I can't keep loving babies like that and having them taken from us. It's just too hard. So, I am going to tell the caseworker that we are done. Done. Take us off the list. We are not willing to take the risk again. Is that right? Do you agree?" I wanted to make sure that we were on the same page.

"Absolutely. This ordeal has crushed us, and we don't want to do it again," John agreed.

Just then, the telephone rang. It was Dawn, our caseworker. "Hi, Julie. It's Dawn. I wanted to call and say I am so sorry that you guys had to go through that. I also wanted to see how you guys are holding up."

"You know, Dawn, it's been really hard." I looked at John and pointed at the phone to let him know that I was going to tell her to take us off the adoption list. "But we are going on as best we can. The thing is, Dawn, we can't do this again."

"Well, that's what I wanted to talk to you about. I know how much you loved that little guy. If, for some reason, the baby comes back into the system, he will immediately be placed with you guys, if you want."

"Of course we want him."

"How do you feel about another placement?" she asked.

"Dawn, we don't want to take another baby and miss the chance to get that baby back." I was obviously saying all the right things because John was nodding next to me.

"Well, you wouldn't have to," she explained.

"I don't understand."

"If you decide to be placed with another baby and Christopher comes back into the system, you would still be called to take him back."

I thought about that for a moment. If we adopted another one and Christopher was returned to us, that would be two kids and we'd be finished building our family. It sounded good to me. Even more than that, it sounded perfect.

"You are sure we would be called when and if Christopher comes back into the system?" I was grasping for some sort of guarantee.

"Yes."

"Okay, then, we are willing to try again," John's head snapped around and he glared at me with bulging eyes, shaking his head wildly. "But only if you are sure…" I waved off John's attempts to get my attention.

"I am positive," she assured me. "Great. You are officially back on the waiting list. If you don't hear from us in a few weeks, call us to remind us that you are still waiting."

I hung up the phone, my heart soaring with the possibility of getting my baby back! In one phone call, I had gone from the boundless abyss to cloud nine, a clear reflection of my emotional instability.

John stared at me. "What was that?"

"Well," I explained, "that was two pieces of good news! The first is that if Christopher comes back into the system for whatever reason, we will be called to take him back. Isn't that great?"

"And the second?" He seemed to doubt that more good news was on the way.

"The second is that we are on the waiting list to be placed again," I said, cautiously.

John just looked at me, dumbstruck.

Hmmm. I guess the news was more exciting when it came from the caseworker herself.

Chapter 37
Premonition

Without any preparation or planning, we managed to secure a table for Valentine's Day, which happened to be on a Friday. There was something rejuvenating about being out of the house, where so many sad memories papered the walls. Dinner for just the two of us turned out to be a surprisingly enjoyable event, given the circumstances of the last few weeks. We sampled food we normally wouldn't eat, reveled in the evening's scheduled entertainment, and amused ourselves with the engrossing act of people watching. One particular couple gestured so wildly that we understood their conversation without hearing any of the words. Almost like our very own sideshow.

We were two people celebrating Valentine's Day, best friends catching up on happenings, and a married couple emerging from their grief. We gorged and chattered and giggled, deep belly laughs that cleansed and healed. All in all, the evening felt like an affirmation that we were going to be all right, something we knew in our heads, of course, but didn't feel in our hearts up until then.

Later, as I lay in bed, I realized I was finally beginning to recover from the loss of our baby. For once, I didn't cry silent tears into my pillow and I didn't experience the dull ache in my chest that developed every night. Instead, I relished the levity that the evening delivered and was grateful to be moving forward. So, prayers said, I drifted into the most relaxing and deepest sleep I could remember in recent months.

And then it happened.

At some point in the middle of the night, in the midst of my dreamless sleep, John grabbed me and shook me. He woke me with an unusual urgency. In my fog, I struggled to understand what he was saying.

"Julie! Julie! I just had a dream, and in my dream we were placed with a baby girl." Even in the moonlight, I could see the earnestness on his face.

"What?"

"Don't you understand? We are getting a baby girl!"

"A baby girl?"

"Yes, I'll tell you all about it in the morning." And quick as that, he rolled over and was sleeping again.

I, on the other hand, could not go back to sleep so easily once I had been awakened, in general. But, the news of a new baby sent the adrenaline pumping throughout my body. My mind raced frantically. *When was she coming? What did she look like? Will she like me?* The questions kept coming and I wanted so badly to wake John and make him answer every one of them, but he was sleeping soundly and said we could talk about it in the morning. *A daughter!* I was over the moon. But then, *oh no, I don't have any girl clothes! And we need to put up the crib!* And then the questions started coming all over again like a recording stuck on repeat.

Sleep must have found me at some point because I woke up while John was in the shower. I sprung out of bed and raced to the kitchen to fix some breakfast. I wanted all obstacles out of the way, so when John came down, he could focus on telling me all about his dream.

That morning it seemed like John emptied the hot water tank. *I mean, save some for the whales, right?* But he finally came down, sat at the table and began eating without saying a word. He had a lot of nerve playing coy about his strange behavior last night, but I was too excited to be annoyed.

I couldn't control myself any longer. So, I finally said, "Start from the beginning and tell me the whole dream."

He just sipped his coffee and looked at me, confused.

"You jerked me out of my sleep to tell me that we were going to be placed with a baby girl, remember?"

He just shook his head again. "Sorry, I don't remember any of that."

I relayed the night's events to him, but he really didn't remember any of it. At first, I was a little disappointed that he didn't have more to tell me, but then it occurred to me that the revelation might have been solely for me. And my heart fluttered.

Chapter 38
Fire Station Baby

Even if John hadn't remembered that he told me we would be placed with a baby girl, I wanted to make sure we were ready this time. When he asked me what I wanted to do that Saturday, I told him I wanted to put up the crib. The crib was on loan to us from my sister, Kathy, and her husband, Mike. It was Mike's crib when he was a baby, and they had used it for their girls when they were babies. Mike's mother had restored the crib and hand painted a beautiful Beatrix Potter Peter Rabbit image on one end. My mom had gifted us with a brand new baby mattress, so all that was needed was some new hardware to assemble it. That meant a trip to Home Depot, which I knew would become an all-day adventure. *I mean, who couldn't find something to love there?*

We did make a day of it, including grabbing a light dinner out, and returned home late in the evening. I checked the phone messages and found that Mary had left me a message. She said that while she was watching the late news, she saw that a woman had left a baby at a local fire station earlier in the evening. "Maybe you could get that baby," she suggested.

I was curious about the details Mary left out. *Was the baby a boy or girl? Which firehouse? Was the woman who left the baby its mother? How old was she? Why would she give up her baby like that?* The story intrigued me, and I had a gob of questions I wanted to ask Mary, but it was after ten o'clock and I was sure that she and her girls were already in bed. I made a mental note to call her before church in the morning.

As it turned out, the story was in the Sunday paper. **"Woman Leaves Baby At Firehouse"** was the headline. The article revealed that a two-day-old infant was left early Saturday evening, but didn't identify the baby's gender. *How did they know the baby was two days old?* The woman who left the baby wouldn't say if she was the baby's mother, only that the baby couldn't be cared for. The writer went on to say that this might have been the first baby left at a fire station since the passage of the Safe Haven Law…. Most of the babies had been left at hospitals…. But this was certainly the first baby to be left in this particular town. *This town was in the jurisdiction of the county in which we lived and through which we were adopting.* … The temperatures were just above freezing, so it would have been unlikely that the baby would have survived if it had been left outdoors….

The phone rang as I finished the article. I put down the paper and picked up the phone.

Mary got right to the point. "Did you get my message last night?"

"Yes, we got home late."

"Did you see the segment on the news this morning?"

"No, but I read about it in the paper."

"Maybe you could call and volunteer to take that baby," she suggested.

"Mary, do you remember how fast we were placed with Christopher? The county has already taken custody of this baby, and I am sure they have already identified some foster parents for this little one. They have emergency staff who can do emergency placements on the weekends. But, thank you for thinking about us." I promised to call her later in the week and we said our good-byes.

Somehow, my other sister and a few of my friends had the same idea, and my phone rang off the hook for the rest of the day. Everyone suggested that I call the county and ask to be placed with that baby. I told each of them the same thing I told Mary and quickly got off the phone. The conversations were a little awkward for me.

The county may have placed that baby already, but may not have as well. The truth was that I didn't want to call and ask. At the beginning of this, I had called and called and called. In fact, I scheduled time on the calendar to remind myself to remind the caseworkers that we were waiting to be placed. I hounded them and look where that got me. I felt like I pushed us into a placement that was doomed from the start, and I wasn't about to do that again. No way. I wasn't calling. I wasn't pushing myself into any more placements. Ever again. Period. I thought about Christopher. It had been weeks since he left and we had heard nothing. All must have been going well in his new foster home with his birth mom. Good for him.

I remembered that I still had his magazine photo on the fridge, one of the four that I had cut out to visualize my goals. I thought about the morning John prayed and felt like we would be placed with the redheaded, blue-eyed boy first. He pointed to the picture. And then, four days later, we were.

I got up and went to the fridge. I pulled the magnet off the magazine photo that looked like Christopher, and circled his face with my finger. He wasn't coming back; I knew that down deep. "I hope you're getting lots of love," I whispered, tears escaping from my eyes.

Then, I turned, and sorrowfully and reluctantly threw the magazine page in the trash.

Chapter 39
A Second Chance

After the calls from my sisters and friends, I followed the local "Fire Station Baby" news with greater interest. As the story developed, it was discovered that the baby surrendered just after dark was a little girl. And in his interview, the captain described the woman who left her as "agitated," but noted that she supplied the firemen with a bottle and formula and diapers to take care of her. The captain called for an ambulance to take the baby to the nearest hospital for examination and then went about taking care of her, which evidently was an easy task, as he said she slept through the whole event.

That little angel's story tugged at my heart, and secretly, I had hoped we could adopt her. From what I had heard about the Safe Haven Law in Colorado, once the baby was left and no one came forward to claim her, she would immediately be placed for adoption. When Monday came and went, however, I lost all hope that we would be placed with the baby left at the firehouse. In my heart, I was certain she was placed with another family. God bless her.

Sickness had kept John home from work on Tuesday morning and by 9:30, we were both sleeping again, he with sickness, me with depression. The phone rang at 10:00. Not just the usual ring, either. It was the stutter tone of a blocked call, which on our phone meant it was either an international call or a call from the county. An important call, in either case. I sprung off the couch, hurdled the coffee table and answered it.

It was Dawn, our caseworker. "Good morning, Julie."

"Good morning, Dawn. How are you?"

"We are good, Dawn. And you?" Greetings out of the way, I hoped she was calling regarding a baby.

"Good. I'm calling you with a placement…." She spoke the sweetest words I had ever heard, and my heart began to race.

She got right down to business. For the next couple minutes, I listened to her explain the baby's situation. Then, I exclaimed, "I'll talk to John and I'll call you back in ten minutes, Dawn. Thank you!"

I threw the phone on the couch and raced up the stairs with an energy my body hadn't ever experienced. I woke John out of his sleep and pestered him until he sat up to clearly hear what I had to say.

"John, that was Dawn from the county. She was calling to place us with that fire station baby! She said that the baby has been at the hospital since Saturday for observation, and right now, it looks like her case will go straight to adoption as no one has come back to claim her. That means no risk, no visits, and no disruptions! Almost the best scenario possible. Can we take her? *Please?*"

John's face was void of emotion, and after a long moment of contemplation, he simply said, "No."

"No?" My heart dropped. *No? Had he not just experienced the heartache of losing a baby? This was a second chance, a new hope. The situation was almost as good as a guarantee!* Maybe he just didn't understand our good fortune here. This was second only to both birth parents signing over their parental rights.

I opened my mouth to try again.

John enjoyed the outward manifestation of my inward struggle long enough and finally offered me relief, "Just kidding. Of course we'll take her."

Oh, that was nasty. It was a good thing I loved him….

Chapter 40
Finally and Forever

We made a quick stop at Target on the way to the hospital. I only had boy clothes at home. I wanted something girlie to dress my daughter in. I ran in alone and picked out two newborn sleepers, one with strawberries and one with pink-and-purple flowers. I could get others later, once she was settled, so I jumped back into the car where my husband waited anxiously.

We were going to meet our forever daughter and bring her home!

We parked in the hospital lot, but instead of getting out immediately, we joined hands and thanked God for this blessing and another shot at parenthood. Somehow, down deep I knew she would be with us permanently.

All legal documents signed, the caseworker turned us over to Jenny, the RN. Jenny gave us a briefing on the baby's short history as a patient in the hospital. "As you probably know, she was brought here by ambulance Saturday night. Her vital signs are good, but her weight was lower than we expected, so we wanted to keep her here a few days to monitor her. She is small, but she is doing well, so she can go home now."

"What were you expecting her weight to be?" It seemed odd to me that they would have any expectation about this baby. The nurse swiped her security badge at the nursery door and a green light flashed. We entered the nursery as she explained. "One of the nurses recognized this baby. This baby was born here, discharged on Saturday, and returned here by ambulance Saturday night. She was small at birth, but has lost a little since."

Another RN, sitting by a crib at the end of the room, cut her explanation short. "Jenny, stop right there. I don't think you should be telling them all of that."

Jenny protested, "I think they deserve to know some of her history."

The other RN, who must have been Jane's superior, walked directly toward Jane and said, "I don't think giving out that information is in the spirit of the Safe Haven Law. I'll take it from here." Then, she turned to us and introduced herself as Rachel, and Jenny left the nursery.

"Come meet your daughter," Rachel motioned us to the crib at the end of the room.

As we approached, John gasped, "Oh, my gosh! Just look at those big, beautiful brown eyes!" Without invitation, he reached down and picked her up.

It was true. This baby had the biggest, most beautiful eyes I had ever seen on a newborn baby. And they were wide open and looking around as if to say, *"Where have you been? I have been waiting for you two forever."*

John held her up over his shoulder and the blanket that swaddled her came loose, exposing her solid pink sleeper. A black marking on the sleeper between her shoulder blades caught my eye and on closer inspection, I saw that someone had written "Property of the Hospital" on the inside. I choked back a tear. It occurred to me that this little angel had nothing in the world—no home, no relatives, not even the clothes on her tiny back. She was indeed an orphan. And for the last few days, she had a carousel of nurses looking after her, a different person at every shift who may only have enough time to feed her and return her to her crib. Not one mom to snuggle her and kiss her and love on her. That was a rough start for a little girl.

Instantly, I wanted to wrap my arms around her and tell her that no one would ever leave her again. I wanted to tell her that I would be the one to fill her hungry tummy, read her animal stories, and tickle her in the bath. I would be the one to celebrate her first Christmas, photograph her first day of kindergarten, and cover her scratches with Band-Aids. And I would be the one to drill her on her spelling words, teach her to cook, and cry at her high school graduation. She may have endured a few rocky days alone, but she would never be alone again.

I would be there.

Chapter 41
Hallelujah!

We secured her in the back of the car and began the twenty-minute ride home.

"Well, what should we name her?" John asked, getting right down to business.

I threw out a few names, none of which John liked. He had attended school or worked with someone who had that name, and for one reason or another, it would not do for his daughter. He, in turn, suggested a couple of names that I also disliked, for the same reasons.

"I don't know right now, but I am sure a name will come to us at some point. All I know is *Hallelujah!* We finally have our forever baby. God answered our prayers." I turned and glanced at the car seat in the back. She ate at the hospital and she was now sleeping soundly, not even a grunt or a grumble.

"That's it! Why don't we name her Halle—as in Hallelujah!? Praise the Lord!" John suggested.

I repeated the name out loud a couple of times, enjoying the way it sounded in my ears. "I think that's perfect. Our little Hallelujah baby...."

When we got home, I called my mom and sisters with our good news. Even though it was a Tuesday, the whole family arrived on our doorstep after work, as I knew they would. We were a curious and supportive bunch. My mom, two sisters, and all four nieces were anxious to meet the newest member of the family, who was passed around to each set of little hands, if only for a few minutes.

Pictures taken and questions answered, I thought it was time for her bath, bottle, and bed. Instead of the sink, I filled a large basin with warm, soapy water, and set it on towels in the middle of the living room floor. My nieces sat circling the "bathtub," and Mary held Halle while Kathy and I gathered clothes and lotion and diapers to dress her. I let Mary and Kathy bathe and feed the baby since they were there, and since I would have plenty of opportunities to do so myself.

Kathy lotioned and dressed Halle, and after brushing her few strands of hair into place, passed her off to Mary for her bottle. The four nieces were getting a little bored at that point and shuffled off to the basement to play.

As I watched them go, I felt happy that Halle would be close to her cousins as well as her aunts and her Nana. Our family was so close. But at the same time, it struck me that she would never know her Papa, my dad, who was so wonderful with children and who adored each of my nieces. His death left a huge hole in my life, and if I could only wish it, I would have wanted him to meet my child. She would be missing a wonderful man.

My thoughts must have shown on my face because Kathy said, "For just having picked up your daughter, you look a little sad." Maybe it was the emotion of the day, but tears sprang readily to my eyes. "I was just thinking about how sad I am that Dad will never know my daughter, and that she will never know him like your girls did."

There was a long pause, and I was a little sorry that I had said anything about it, bringing down the happiness in the room. But Kathy thoughtfully responded, "He won't know her here, but he knew her in heaven before she came to you...."

That statement caused the tears to flood my eyes. I imagined that in heaven my Dad rocked Halle in his strong arms and gently kissed her on her forehead before sending her to earth to be a blessing to me. It was the most wonderful image I'd ever had.

I recognized that her words may not have been accurate or doctrinally correct or might have even sounded ridiculous to some, but I clung to them with the hope that they were true.... I believed that they could be true.... I had faith that they were true.... And after all, faith is the substance of things hoped for...

The Beginning

Sneak a peek at the sequel to
Fire Station Baby

Halle's Brother?

It had happened a few days before—relatively old news—but I was still hooked.

The day it occurred, and the following, it was covered by all three local news programs and I switched from station to station for any new scrap of information I could glean. Now, there was barely any mention of the story at all. The reporters had moved on to current happenings around town, but I was stuck.

I switched off the television and set the remote on top of it. Halle was taking a rare nap up in her crib and I was lost in my thoughts. Not lost exactly—more like conflicted.

Two-and-a-half years earlier, my daughter was surrendered to that firehouse by her birth mother. And now, another newborn baby had been left at that same firehouse. Was it just a coincidence? Maybe. Maybe not.

What if this new baby was her biological sibling? John and I already had Halle and another baby we were fostering and hoping to adopt. Would a third so soon be too much for us? Did it matter when this baby could be her sibling? Was the fact that two babies were left anonymously at the same firehouse a coincidence or a connection? I thought it was a connection, but was that enough "evidence" to take to the county?

I finally decided that I didn't care if the county workers thought I was crazy. I was going to ask.

I picked up the telephone and dialed Karen. I couldn't quite pin down the feeling I had in my stomach. It was a cross between elation and nausea, the same feeling I got when I had to speak to a crowd. Only this time, there was so much more at stake.

The phone rang three times and just as I was preparing to leave a message, Karen picked up.

"Karen, how are you? It's Julie! How are your girls?" Karen had adopted two biological girls herself shortly after we were placed with Halle. I heard the pride in her voice as she spoke about their developments and bonding.

She finished and asked me about Halle and our newest foster baby. I quickly gave her an update and then got to the purpose of my call.

"Karen, I think the baby left at the fire station the other day might be Halle's biological sibling," I blurted out.
Karen went silent.

I had been contemplating this for a couple of days and the more I dwelled on it, the more certain I grew. I knew it in my head; I knew it in my heart; and I knew it in my bones. Any actual proof would be superfluous. I felt it deeply, therefore it must be true. Period. It was my modus operandi. However, I sometimes had to connect the dots for other people.

"Karen, think about it. Two babies who are the same ethnicity are left at the same fire station two years apart. No two babies have ever been left at the same fire station. I think their birth mother might have wanted them to be together." Was I trying to convince myself or her?

"Was it the same fire station?" she asked.

"Yes."

She hesitated for a moment, thinking about the ramifications. "Julie, that baby has already been placed in foster care with another couple. You can't have all the fire station babies left in our county. You just can't."

The elation and nausea left me suddenly and what arose was anger. "Karen, I don't want all of the fire station babies in the county, but I do want this one if he is her biological sibling." I spoke slowly, hoping to keep the anger in check. I continued, "Isn't it the county's policy to keep siblings together whenever possible?"

"The baby left at the fire station is of XXXXXX ethnicity," she said.

"So is Halle."

"That baby was premature and had low birth weight."
"So did Halle."

She was silent for a long moment. "Julie, here is what I can do for you. I can give you the names of the couple who were placed with that baby and you can keep the kids in contact that way. That's the best I can offer you. We're not moving him now."

This was unbelievable! How many times had the county preached that it wanted to keep biological siblings together whenever possible? My daughter possibly had a biological sibling out there who had not yet been adopted and this caseworker was telling me I can't have that baby because he's already with another foster couple? The county doesn't want to take the baby from them so he could be with his sister—the only biological connection he might ever have? They might have to admit they were wrong?

By nature, I was not a confrontational person. But something fierce rose up in me and by then I was shaking. Again, I spoke slowly and clearly, "No, Karen, I want a DNA test done on both children to prove or disprove a biological connection. And if there is one, I am telling you now, we want that child."

There was a long, tense silence.

"Let me call you back," she finally said.

Julie may be contacted at
www.firestationbaby.com